The Birdwatcher's Book of Lists

The Birdwatcher's Book of Lists

LISTS FOR RECREATION AND RECORDKEEPING

DR. LESTER L. SHORT

Curator and Chairman, Department of Ornithology
American Museum of Natural History

Illustrations by
JUAN LUIS G. VELA

Alfred A. Knopf

New York 1987

This is a Borzoi Book
published by Alfred A. Knopf, Inc.

Library of Congress Cataloging-in-Publication Data

Short, Lester L.
The birdwatcher's book of lists. Eastern region.

1. Bird watching—United States. 2. Bird watching—
Atlantic States. 3. Bird watching—Middle West.
4. Bird watching—Canada, Eastern. 5. Birds—United
States. 6. Birds—Atlantic States. 7. Birds—Middle
West. 8. Birds—Canada, Eastern. 1. Vela, Juan Luis G.
II. Title.
QL682.S54   1987   598'.07'23474   86-46017
ISBN 0-394-75197-3 (pbk.)

Prepared and produced by Running Heads Incorporated, New York.
Editor: Mary E. Forsell
Art Director/Designer: Gael Towey
Original Paintings: Juan Luis G. Vela
Map Art: Michele Lerner

Color reproductions by Hong Kong Scanner Craft Company Ltd.
Printed and bound in Hong Kong by Leefung-Asco Printers Ltd.
Typeset by David E. Seham Assoc. Inc., Typographers

First Printing

Companion volume: *The Birdwatcher's Book of Lists: Western
Region,* by Dr. Lester L. Short.

The author thanks Jennifer F.M. Horne,
Mary Forsell, and Marta Hallett
for their helpful suggestions,
and Jennifer, especially, for her patience.

. . . .

This book is dedicated to all those working to
save birds and their habitats for posterity;
to the extent that we succeed,
those following will lead a richer life.

Contents

Introduction

PART
1

The Birding Lists

PART

2

The Maps

Resident, Wintering,
and Breeding Ranges **1 1 0**

. . . .

APPENDIX SOURCES

This book of lists has been designed so that every birder can better organize and enjoy his or her birdwatching activities. The lists have been created to correspond to natural categories, in an effort to assist the birder in making correct identifications, and keeping a permanent record of these, and to educate the birder to other facets of ornithology. The lists in and of themselves, and the categories they represent, tell much about birds: their seasonality, plumage variations, and habitats. In fact, each list here has been organized so that it brings to the birder an understanding of natural groupings of birds, based variously on a common habitat; a particular group of birds that act in a particular way; a single family, order, or genus of birds; the time of day, month, or year, when a group of birds engages in a particular activity; or the changing plumages of birds, based on the season of the year.

Rather than overwhelm the reader with illustrations that attempt to identify every species included here, we have chosen instead to portray only the more common, widespread, and conspicuous birds of the region covered; that is, the area of North America north of Mexico and east of the 100th meridian. We realize that any experienced birder would have his own selection of such species; this being the author's own. This book is *not* a field guide. In fact, it is an ancillary tool, one that should be used alongside any of the fine field guides available to the birder today.

The twenty-three lists offered here present common, regularly occurring species, and generally exclude unusual or uncommon birds. In dealing with less common species, the principle for the birder to follow is to consider a bird to represent the expected, common species *unless* it can be proved by its features that it is not such. The unexpected *can* happen; but birding, like any other science, generally works within the law of averages, so it should be presumed that the species sighted is the most common one.

This book has been written with the assumption that the

birder will be viewing for the lists from one location. However, our range delineation—that is, north of Mexico east of the 100th meridian in North America—may change some species from "expected" to "unexpected." To help the birder cope with sightings with as much precision as possible, the symbols *N* for north, *S* for south, *E* for east, and *W* for west have been used. These symbols, in parentheses following the English name of the bird on the list, show restriction in occurrence of a species to the part of the region so specified.

The twenty-three lists have been compiled in an order that moves from the commoner, most conspicuous, species, to the most difficult, or those that would necessitate travel from a home environment for completion. This should help the birder to familiarize himself or herself with the techniques of birding, feel the accomplishment of compiling the lists, and move on, with ease, to the more ambitious, difficult lists.

Each of the lists here that has no designated time limitation—that is, in hours or season, for sightings—are presumed to be compiled in a single sighting period, for which the reader will set his or her own time frame. The larger lists relating to habitat are generally exclusive. In other words, a woodland species that enters overgrown pastures will be listed here as a "woodland" rather than a "field" bird. Some birds of open areas that enter open woodlands will be found on the "field" bird list. Those lists that deal with migrant species, as well as the *24-Hour Spring Field Birdwatch* list, involve selecting the most opportune time, or season, for the sighting. In the northeast, for example, mid-May and mid-September provide the seasons with the greatest range of available species. Farther south, in the southeast, the sightings must be accomplished earlier, in April, or even March, for example, to fall into the period considered as the "Spring" season for birds. In terms of time of day for compilation, the *24-Hour Spring Field Birdwatch* list should begin in the dark, in order to be able to spot the widest range of nightbirds. Some birders begin a twenty-four hour watch at 2:00 or 3:00 AM, for example.

The list of *Female Waterfowl* includes fairly common

species that have a distinctive female plumage. The *Immature Birds* species are also those with plumages that are distinct and carried by the birds for a long period: This may be a period of months in smaller birds; or years in some of the larger species. Note that most birds have two non-adult plumages, immature and juvenile, and some even have a downy young plumage. The downy plumage, however, is usually held for a short period, often only when the young are with their parents, so their identities can be discerned by their parents. Also o-mitted from the listing of immature birds are those young birds that essentially resemble the adult female so closely that they cannot be readily distinguished from her. It is interesting to note that most immature-plumaged birds show a greater resemblance to the adult female than the adult male, no matter which gender the offspring. The restricted lists, such as *Birds of Prey,* are based on frequently seen species that, in the cases of restriction, are only found in the specified area, or habitat.

Flight identification presents completely different problems for the birder than does the identification of perched species, so included here is a list for completion of those birds that are commonly seen in flight. In the list for *Canadian Border and Mountain Birds,* the symbols *Su* for summer, or breeding, and *Wi* for winter, or nonbreeding, plumages are used.

The *Vagrant Species* list has been designed as a personal tally, for which species are "vagrant" depends on the birder's location for sighting. Irregular events, such as hurricanes, which occur in diverse places, depending on their paths, can bring birds in from afar, but these events vary tremendously in terms of the birds that will be accidentally carried along and, fortunately, major hurricanes are not annual events.

Arctic birds, as defined here, are those species from the high Arctic that do not breed in southern Canada. These birds should be sought in winter, and are generally more likely to be observed in the north than in the south. Night birding should take place during the breeding season, in order to be able to sight the greatest number of species, in that these birds are more plentiful at this time of year. The breeding season for these birds generally means June in the north, but may occur as early as April in the deep south.

The *North American Travel* and *World Travel* lists have been designed to be constructed entirely by the reader. The source for the species in these lists should be the birder's field guide. Rather than catalogue some 9,000 species worldwide or the approximately 840 in North America alone, it is more expedient to allow the reader to compile a personal list.

In addition to the twenty-three lists, a section containing range maps has been included in the book, so that the reader can more precisely verify, by locale, whether a bird has been accurately sighted. Range information—incorporating habitat resident, and winter patterns—can be one of the key factors in making a positive identification. Only rarely will a bird stray from its known habitat and flight pattern. The range maps here are meant to present a diverse array of the different patterns of distribution of birds, including residents, migrants that winter in a part of their breeding range, migrants that move over long distances, and wintering species.

In addition to the lists, illustrations, and range map information, also included is an "Appendix" that provides references, lists of Audubon Societies and addresses, and popular bird-watching periodicals.

English and scientific names used in the listings conform to the 1983 *American Ornithologists' Union Check-list of North American Birds,* Sixth Edition.

As mentioned previously, a good field guide is a necessity for every birdwatcher, and one must be used in conjunction with this book. Some excellent guides are available, including those that pertain to states, or even particular localities. A listing of these can be found in the bibliography in the *Appendix.*

In trying to identify a species, note, and jot down, if possible, all the visible characteristics *before* the bird disappears from sight. A micro-cassette recorder is a great help, for one can whisper characteristics without taking one's eyes from the bird. In addition to general color and size, try to determine the color of beak, legs, feet, and undertail feathers. Notice whether the bird has wing bars, an eye-ring, white on its tail; stripes on its body, a patch on its cheek, or a line over its eyes. Check the shape of its bill. Notice the size, habits, and habitats, and voice of the bird. Any one of these can be an important clue to the identity of the species. In many cases, the bird's English or scientific name is descriptive of one of these factors.

It is our hope that this book will assist you in enjoying North America's birds. Birdwatching is a lifelong "occupation," providing many thrills and enhancing the understanding of man's place in nature. Enjoy your birds and help as you can to preserve their habitats, for throughout the world, and especially in the tropics, we stand to lose for all time, great numbers of species that those coming after us will never see and know. As our understanding of birds grows on a popular level, the greater will be our ability to preserve all the species for viewing by following generations.

LESTER L. SHORT

The Birding Lists

Birdfeeder Birds

PLACE

. . . .

SPECIES SIGHTED

. . . .

NUMBER

SPECIES SIGHTED

♂ ♀ JUV. IMM. **D O V E S**

—— —— —— —— Mourning Dove, *Zenaida macroura*

—— —— —— —— Common Ground-Dove(S), *Columbina passerina*

H U M M I N G B I R D S

—— —— —— —— Ruby-throated Hummingbird, *Archilochus colubris*

W O O D P E C K E R S

—— —— —— —— Red-headed Woodpecker, *Melanerpes erythrocephalus*

—— —— —— —— Red-bellied Woodpecker, *Melanerpes carolinus*

—— —— —— —— Downy Woodpecker, *Picoides pubescens*

—— —— —— —— Hairy Woodpecker, *Picoides villosus*

—— —— —— —— Northern Flicker, *Colaptes auratus*

JAYS AND CROWS	♂	♀	JUV.	IMM.
Blue Jay, *Cyanocitta cristata*				
Scrub Jay(S), *Aphelocoma coerulescens*				
American Crow, *Corvus brachyrhynchos*				

CHICKADEES AND TITMICE

Black-capped Chickadee, *Parus atricapillus*				
Carolina Chickadee(S), *Parus carolinensis*				
Boreal Chickadee(N), *Parus hudsonicus*				
Tufted Titmouse, *Parus bicolor*				

♂	♀	JUV.	IMM.	NUTHATCHES AND WRENS
___	___	___	___	White-breasted Nuthatch, *Sitta carolinensis*
___	___	___	___	House Wren, *Troglodytes aedon*

THRUSHES AND MOCKINGBIRDS

___	___	___	___	Eastern Bluebird, *Sialia sialis*
___	___	___	___	American Robin, *Turdus migratorius*
___	___	___	___	Northern Mockingbird, *Mimus polyglottos*

STARLINGS

___	___	___	___	European Starling, *Sturnus vulgaris*

CARDINALS GROSBEAKS, AND BUNTINGS

___	___	___	___	Northern Cardinal, *Cardinalis cardinalis*
___	___	___	___	Rose-breasted Grosbeak, *Pheucticus ludovicianus*
___	___	___	___	Painted Bunting(S), *Passerina ciris*

TOWHEES, SPARROWS, AND JUNCOS

___	___	___	___	Rufous-sided Towhee, *Pipilo erythrophthalmus*
___	___	___	___	American Tree Sparrow(N), *Spizella arborea*
___	___	___	___	Chipping Sparrow, *Spizella passerina*
___	___	___	___	Field Sparrow, *Spizella pusilla*

	♂	♀	JUV.	IMM.
Fox Sparrow, *Passerella iliaca*	___	___	___	___
Song Sparrow, *Melospiza melodia*	___	___	___	___
White-throated Sparrow, *Zonotrichia albicollis*	___	___	___	___
White-crowned Sparrow, *Zonotrichia leucophrys*	___	___	___	___
Dark-eyed Junco, *Junco hyemalis*	___	___	___	___

BLACKBIRDS AND ALLIES

	♂	♀	JUV.	IMM.
Red-winged Blackbird, *Agelaius phoeniceus*	___	___	___	___
Boat-tailed Grackle, *Quiscalus major*	___	___	___	___
Common Grackle, *Quiscalus quiscula*	___	___	___	___
Brown-headed Cowbird, *Molothrus ater*	___	___	___	___

FINCHES AND ALLIES

	♂	♀	JUV.	IMM.
Purple Finch, *Carpodacus purpureus*	___	___	___	___
House Finch, *Carpodacus mexicanus*	___	___	___	___
Common Redpoll(N), *Carduelis flammea*	___	___	___	___
Pine Siskin, *Carduelis pinus*	___	___	___	___
American Goldfinch, *Carduelis tristis*	___	___	___	___
Evening Grosbeak(N), *Coccothraustes verpertinus*	___	___	___	___
House Sparrow, *Passer domesticus*	___	___	___	___

**Month-
by-
Month
Backyard
Birdwatch**

FOR YEAR

. . . .

AT

. . . .

P L A C E

J A N U A R Y

_____ _____ _____

_____ _____ _____

_____ _____ _____

F E B R U A R Y

_____ _____ _____

_____ _____ _____

_____ _____ _____

M A R C H

_____ _____ _____

_____ _____ _____

_____ _____ _____

A P R I L

_____ _____ _____

_____ _____ _____

_____ _____ _____

M A Y

_____ _____ _____

_____ _____ _____

_____ _____ _____

J U N E

_____ _____ _____

_____ _____ _____

_____ _____ _____

JULY

_____ _____ _____

_____ _____ _____

_____ _____ _____

_____ _____ _____

AUGUST

_____ _____ _____

_____ _____ _____

_____ _____ _____

_____ _____ _____

SEPTEMBER

_____ _____ _____

_____ _____ _____

_____ _____ _____

_____ _____ _____

O C T O B E R

_____ _____ _____

_____ _____ _____

_____ _____ _____

_____ _____ _____

N O V E M B E R

_____ _____ _____

_____ _____ _____

_____ _____ _____

_____ _____ _____

D E C E M B E R

_____ _____ _____

_____ _____ _____

_____ _____ _____

_____ _____ _____

Nesting Yard Species

SPECIES SIGHTED

(Fill in ♂, ♀, Juv., or Imm.)

DOVES

_____ Mourning Dove, *Zenaida macroura*

_____ Common Ground-Dove, *Columbina passerina*

WOODPECKERS

_____ Red-headed Woodpecker, *Melanerpes erythrocephalus*

_____ Red-bellied Woodpecker, *Melanerpes carolinus*

_____ Downy Woodpecker, *Picoides pubescens*

_____ Northern Flicker, *Colaptes auratus*

SWALLOWS, JAYS, AND CROWS

_____ Purple Martin, *Progne subis*

_____ Tree Swallow, *Tachycineta bicolor*

_____ Barn Swallow, *Hirundo rustica*

_____ Blue Jay, *Cyanocitta cristata*

_____ American Crow, *Corvus brachyrhynchos*

CHICKADEES, TITMICE, NUTHATCHES, WRENS, AND THRUSHES

_____ Black-capped Chickadee, *Parus atricapillus*

Carolina Chickadee (S), *Parus carolinensis* _____

Tufted Titmouse, *Parus bicolor* _____

Red-breasted Nuthatch, *Sitta canadensis* _____

Carolina Wren, *Thryothorus ludovicianus* _____

House Wren, *Troglodytes aedon* _____

Eastern Bluebird, *Sialia sialis* _____

Wood Thrush, *Hylocichla mustelina* _____

American Robin, *Turdus migratorius* _____

MOCKINGBIRDS AND ALLIES

Gray Catbird, *Dumetella carolinensis* _____

Northern Mockingbird, *Mimus polyglottos* _____

Brown Thrasher, *Toxostoma rufum* _____

European Starling, *Sturnus vulgarls* _____

CARDINALS AND ALLIES

Northern Cardinal, *Cardinalis cardinalis* _____

Rose-breasted Grosbeak, *Pheucticus ludovicianus* _____

Painted Bunting, *Passerina ciris* _____

Rufous-sided Towhee, *Pipilo erythrophthalmus* _____

Chipping Sparrow, *Spizella passerina* _____

Song Sparrow, *Melospiza melodia* _____

BLACKBIRDS, ORIOLES, FINCHES, AND ALLIES

Common Grackle, *Quiscalus quiscula* _____

Brown-headed Cowbird, *Molothrus ater* _____

Orchard Oriole (S), *Icterus spurius* _____

Northern Oriole, *Icterus galbula* _____

House Finch, *Carpodacus mexicanus* _____

House Sparrow, *Passer domesticus* _____

COMMENTS AND SIGHTING NOTES

. . . .

Coastal Waterbirds

DATE	SPECIES SIGHTED
. . . .	

PLACE

. . . .

SPECIES SIGHTED

. . . .

NUMBER

   ♂   ♀   JUV. IMM. LOONS AND GREBES

___ ___ ___ ___ Red-throated Loon, *Gavia stellata*

___ ___ ___ ___ Common Loon, *Gavia immer*

___ ___ ___ ___ Horned Grebe, *Podiceps auritus*

___ ___ ___ ___ Red-necked Grebe, *Podiceps grisegena*

PELICANS AND CORMORANTS

___ ___ ___ ___ Brown Pelican(S), *Pelecanus occidentalis*

___ ___ ___ ___ Great Cormorant(N), *Phalacrocorax carbo*

___ ___ ___ ___ Double-crested Cormorant, *Phalacrocorax auritus*

HERONS, IBISES, AND SPOONBILLS	♂	♀	JUV.	IMM.
Great Blue Heron, *Ardea herodias*				
Great Egret, *Casmerodius albus*				
Snowy Egret, *Egretta thula*				
Tricolored Heron(S), *Egretta tricolor*				
Reddish Egret(S), *Egretta rufescens*				
Black-crowned Night-Heron, *Nycticorax nycticorax*				
Yellow-crowned Night-Heron, *Nycticorax violaceus*				
White Ibis(S), *Eudocimus albus*				
Glossy Ibis, *Plegadis falcinellus*				
Roseate Spoonbill(S), *Ajaia ajaja*				

♂	♀	JUV.	IMM.	SWANS, GEESE, AND DUCKS
___	___	___	___	Mute Swan(N), *Cygnus olor*
___	___	___	___	Brant, *Branta bernicla*
___	___	___	___	Canada Goose(N), *Branta canadensis*
___	___	___	___	American Black Duck(N), *Anas rubripes*
___	___	___	___	Northern Shoveler, *Anas clypeata*
___	___	___	___	Canvasback, *Aythya valisineria*
___	___	___	___	Redhead, *Aythya americana*
___	___	___	___	Greater Scaup, *Aythya marila*
___	___	___	___	Lesser Scaup, *Aythya affinis*
___	___	___	___	Common Eider, *Somateria mollissima*
___	___	___	___	King Eider(N), *Somateria spectabilis*
___	___	___	___	Harlequin Duck(N), *Histrionicus histrionicus*
___	___	___	___	Oldsquaw(N), *Clangula hyemalis*
___	___	___	___	Black Scoter(N), *Melanitta nigra*
___	___	___	___	Surf Scoter, *Melanitta perspicillata*
___	___	___	___	White-winged Scoter, *Melanitta fusca*
___	___	___	___	Common Goldeneye, *Bucephala clangula*
___	___	___	___	Barrow's Goldeneye(N), *Bucephala islandica*
___	___	___	___	Bufflehead, *Bucephala albeola*
___	___	___	___	Common Merganser, *Mergus merganser*
___	___	___	___	Red-breasted Merganser, *Mergus serrator*
___	___	___	___	Ruddy Duck, *Oxyura jamaicensis*

EAGLES AND HAWKS	♂	♀	JUV.	IMM.
Bald Eagle, *Haliaeetus leucocephalus*	___	___	___	___
Northern Harrier, *Circus cyaneus*	___	___	___	___

. . . .

RAILS, GALLINULES, COOTS, AND LIMPKINS				
Black Rail, *Laterallus jamaicensis*	___	___	___	___
Clapper Rail, *Rallus longirostris*	___	___	___	___
Virginia Rail, *Rallus limicola*	___	___	___	___
Sora, *Porzana carolina*	___	___	___	___
Common Moorhen, *Gallinula chloropus*	___	___	___	___
American Coot, *Fulica americana*	___	___	___	___
Limpkin(S), *Aramus guarauna*	___	___	___	___

PLOVERS, OYSTERCATCHERS, SANDPIPERS, AND ALLIES				
Black-bellied Plover, *Pluvialis squatarola*	___	___	___	___
Wilson's Plover, *Charadrius wilsonia*	___	___	___	___
Piping Plover, *Charadrius melodus*	___	___	___	___
Killdeer, *Charadrius vociferus*	___	___	___	___
American Oystercatcher, *Haematopus palliatus*	___	___	___	___

♂	♀	JUV.	IMM.	
⎯	⎯	⎯	⎯	Greater Yellowlegs, *Tringa melanoleuca*
⎯	⎯	⎯	⎯	Lesser Yellowlegs, *Tringa flavipes*
⎯	⎯	⎯	⎯	Willet, *Catoptrophorus semipalmatus*
⎯	⎯	⎯	⎯	Spotted Sandpiper, *Actitis macularia*
⎯	⎯	⎯	⎯	Ruddy Turnstone, *Arenaria interpres*
⎯	⎯	⎯	⎯	Red Knot, *Calidris canutus*
⎯	⎯	⎯	⎯	Sanderling, *Calidris alba*
⎯	⎯	⎯	⎯	Semipalmated Sandpiper, *Calidris pusilla*
⎯	⎯	⎯	⎯	Western Sandpiper, *Calidris mauri*
⎯	⎯	⎯	⎯	Least Sandpiper, *Calidris minutilla*
⎯	⎯	⎯	⎯	Purple Sandpiper, *Calidris maritima*
⎯	⎯	⎯	⎯	Dunlin, *Calidris alpina*
⎯	⎯	⎯	⎯	Curlew Sandpiper, *Calidris ferruginea*
⎯	⎯	⎯	⎯	Short-billed Dowitcher, *Limnodromus griseus*
⎯	⎯	⎯	⎯	Common Snipe, *Gallinago gallinago*

GULLS, TERNS, AND SKIMMERS

♂	♀	JUV.	IMM.	
⎯	⎯	⎯	⎯	Laughing Gull(S), *Larus atricilla*
⎯	⎯	⎯	⎯	Ring-billed Gull, *Larus delawarensis*
⎯	⎯	⎯	⎯	Herring Gull, *Larus argentatus*
⎯	⎯	⎯	⎯	Ivory Gull, *Pagophila eburnea*
⎯	⎯	⎯	⎯	Caspian Tern, *Sterna caspia*
⎯	⎯	⎯	⎯	Common Tern, *Sterna hirundo*

	♂	♀	JUV.	IMM.
Least Tern, *Sterna antillarum*	___	___	___	___
Black Tern, *Chlidonias niger*	___	___	___	___
Black Skimmer, *Rynchops niger*	___	___	___	___

OWLS AND KINGFISHERS

Short-eared Owl, *Asio flammeus*	___	___	___	___
Belted Kingfisher, *Ceryle alcyon*	___	___	___	___

SWALLOWS AND CROWS

Barn Swallow, *Hirundo rustica*	___	___	___	___
Fish Crow, *Corvus ossifragus*	___	___	___	___

WRENS

Marsh Wren, *Cistothorus palustris*	___	___	___	___

SPARROWS

Savannah Sparrow, *Passerculus sandwichensis*	___	___	___	___
Sharp-tailed Sparrow, *Ammodramus caudacutus*	___	___	___	___
Seaside Sparrow, *Ammodramus maritimus*	___	___	___	___

BLACKBIRDS

Red-winged Blackbird(S), *Agelaius phoeniceus*	___	___	___	___
Boat-tailed Grackle, *Quiscalus major*	___	___	___	___
Common Grackle, *Quiscalus quiscula*	___	___	___	___

Inland Waterbirds

DATE

. . . .

PLACE

. . . .

SPECIES SIGHTED

. . . .

NUMBER

SPECIES SIGHTED

♂ ♀ JUV. IMM.

LOONS AND GREBES

__ __ __ __ Common Loon, *Gavia immer*

__ __ __ __ Pied-billed Grebe, *Podilymbus podiceps*

__ __ __ __ Horned Grebe, *Podiceps auritus*

__ __ __ __ Western Grebe(W), *Aechmophorus occidentalis*

CORMORANTS AND DARTERS

__ __ __ __ Double-crested Cormorant(N), *Phalacrocorax auritus*

__ __ __ __ Anhinga(S), *Anhinga anhinga*

BITTERNS, HERONS, IBISES, AND STORKS

	♂	♀	JUV.	IMM.
American Bittern, *Botaurus lentiginosus*	___	___	___	___
Least Bittern, *Ixobrychus exilis*	___	___	___	___
Great Blue Heron, *Ardea herodias*	___	___	___	___
Great Egret, *Casmerodius albus*	___	___	___	___
Snowy Egret, *Egretta thula*	___	___	___	___
Little Blue Heron, *Egretta caerulea*	___	___	___	___
Cattle Egret, *Bubulcus ibis*	___	___	___	___
Green-backed Heron, *Butorides striatus*	___	___	___	___

♂	♀	JUV.	IMM.	
___	___	___	___	Black-crowned Night-Heron, *Nycticorax nycticorax*
___	___	___	___	Yellow-crowned Night-Heron, *Nycticorax violaceus*
___	___	___	___	Glossy Ibis, *Plegadis falcinellus*
___	___	___	___	Wood Stork(S), *Mycteria americana*

SWANS, GEESE, AND DUCKS

___	___	___	___	Tundra Swan, *Cygnus columbianus*
___	___	___	___	Mute Swan, *Cygnus olor*
___	___	___	___	Snow Goose, *Chen caerulescens*
___	___	___	___	Canada Goose(N), *Branta canadensis*
___	___	___	___	Wood Duck, *Aix sponsa*
___	___	___	___	Green-winged Teal, *Anas crecca*
___	___	___	___	American Black Duck(N), *Anas rubripes*
___	___	___	___	Mallard, *Anas platyrhynchos*
___	___	___	___	Northern Pintail, *Anas acuta*
___	___	___	___	Blue-winged Teal, *Anas discors*
___	___	___	___	Northern Shoveler, *Anas clypeata*
___	___	___	___	Gadwall, *Anas strepera*
___	___	___	___	American Wigeon, *Anas americana*
___	___	___	___	Canvasback, *Aythya valisineria*
___	___	___	___	Redhead, *Aythya americana*
___	___	___	___	Ring-necked Duck, *Aythya collaris*
___	___	___	___	Greater Scaup, *Aythya marila*
___	___	___	___	Lesser Scaup, *Aythya affinis*

	♂	♀	JUV.	IMM.

White-winged Scoter, *Melanitta fusca* _____ _____ _____ _____

Common Goldeneye, *Bucephala clangula* _____ _____ _____ _____

Bufflehead (N), *Bucephala albeola* _____ _____ _____ _____

Hooded Merganser, *Lophodytes cucullatus* _____ _____ _____ _____

Common Merganser, *Mergus merganser* _____ _____ _____ _____

Ruddy Duck, *Oxyura jamaicensis* _____ _____ _____ _____

KITES, EAGLES, HAWKS, AND ALLIES

Osprey, *Pandion haliaetus* _____ _____ _____ _____

Bald Eagle, *Haliaeetus leucocephalus* _____ _____ _____ _____

Northern Harrier, *Circus cyaneus* _____ _____ _____ _____

RAILS, COOTS, LIMPKINS, AND CRANES

Yellow Rail, *Coturnicops noveboracensis* _____ _____ _____ _____

King Rail, *Rallus elegans* _____ _____ _____ _____

Virginia Rail, *Rallus limicola* _____ _____ _____ _____

Sora, *Porzana carolina* _____ _____ _____ _____

Common Moorhen, *Gallinula chloropus* _____ _____ _____ _____

American Coot, *Fulica americana* _____ _____ _____ _____

Limpkin (S), *Aramus guarauna* _____ _____ _____ _____

♂	♀	JUV.	IMM.	PLOVERS, SANDPIPERS, AND ALLIES
___	___	___	___	Sandhill Crane, *Grus canadensis*
___	___	___	___	Black-bellied Plover, *Pluvialis squatarola*
___	___	___	___	Lesser Golden-Plover, *Pluvialis apricaria*
___	___	___	___	Killdeer, *Charadrius vociferus*
___	___	___	___	Greater Yellowlegs, *Tringa melanoleuca*
___	___	___	___	Lesser Yellowlegs, *Tringa flavipes*
___	___	___	___	Spotted Sandpiper, *Actitis macularia*
___	___	___	___	Whimbrel, *Numenius phaeopus*
___	___	___	___	Semipalmated Sandpiper, *Calidris pusilla*
___	___	___	___	Western Sandpiper, *Calidris mauri*
___	___	___	___	Dunlin, *Calidris alpina*
___	___	___	___	Short-billed Dowitcher, *Limnodromus griseus*

GULLS AND TERNS

♂	♀	JUV.	IMM.	
___	___	___	___	Ring-billed Gull, *Larus delawarensis*
___	___	___	___	Herring Gull, *Larus argentatus*
___	___	___	___	Common Tern, *Sterna hirundo*
___	___	___	___	Least Tern, *Sterna antillarum*
___	___	___	___	Black Tern, *Chlidonias niger*

KINGFISHERS   ♂   ♀   JUV.   IMM.

Belted Kingfisher, *Ceryle alcyon* ___ ___ ___ ___

FLYCATCHERS
AND SWALLOWS

Alder Flycatcher, *Empidonax* ___ ___ ___ ___
alnorum

Tree Swallow, *Tachycineta* ___ ___ ___ ___
bicolor

Bank Swallow, *Riparia riparia* ___ ___ ___ ___

Rough-Winged Swallow, ___ ___ ___ ___
Stelgidopteryx ruficollis

Barn Swallow, *Hirundo* ___ ___ ___ ___
rustica

PIPITS

Water Pipit, *Anthus spinoletta* ___ ___ ___ ___

WARBLERS

Northern Waterthrush, *Seiurus* ___ ___ ___ ___
noveboracensis

Common Yellowthroat, ___ ___ ___ ___
Geothlypis trichas

SPARROWS

Song Sparrow, *Melospiza* ___ ___ ___ ___
melodia

Lincoln's Sparrow, *Melospiza* ___ ___ ___ ___
lincolnii

Swamp Sparrow, *Melospiza* ___ ___ ___ ___
georgiana

BLACKBIRDS

Red-winged Blackbird, ___ ___ ___ ___
Agelaius phoeniceus

Rusty Blackbird, *Euphagus* ___ ___ ___ ___
carolinus

**COMMENTS
AND
SIGHTING
NOTES**

. . . .

Female
Waterfowl

DATE

. . . .

PLACE

. . . .

SPECIES
SIGHTED

. . . .

N U M B E R

GENUS *Aix*
_____ Wood Duck, *Aix sponsa*

GENUS *Anas*
_____ Green-winged Teal, *Anas crecca*
_____ Mallard, *Anas platyrhynchos*
_____ Northern Pintail, *Anas acuta*
_____ Blue-winged Teal, *Anas discors*
_____ Northern Shoveler, *Anas clypeata*
_____ Gadwall, *Anas strepera*
_____ American Wigeon, *Anas americana*

GENUS *Aythya*
_____ Canvasback, *Aythya valisineria*
_____ Redhead, *Aythya americana*

Ring-necked Duck, *Aythya collaris* _____

Greater Scaup, *Aythya marila* _____

Lesser Scaup, *Aythya affinis* _____

GENUS *Somateria*
Common Eider, *Somateria mollissima* _____

GENUS *Clangula*
Oldsquaw(N), *Clangula hyemalis* _____

GENUS *Melanitta*
Black Scoter, *Melanitta nigra* _____

Surf Scoter, *Melanitta perspicillata* _____

White-winged Scoter, *Melanitta fusca* _____

GENUS *Bucephala*
Common Goldeneye, *Bucephala clangula* _____

Bufflehead(N), *Bucephala albeola* _____

GENUS *Lophodytes*
Hooded Merganser, *Lophodytes cucullatus* _____

GENUS *Mergus*
Common Merganser, *Mergus merganser* _____

Red-breasted Merganser, *Mergus serrator* _____

GENUS *Oxyura*
Ruddy Duck, *Oxyura jamaicensis* _____

COMMENTS AND SIGHTING NOTES

. . . .

SPECIES SIGHTED

Immature Birds

♂ ♀ GANNETS, PELICANS, HERONS, AND SWANS

___ ___ Northern Gannet(N), *Sula bassanus*

___ ___ Brown Pelican(S), *Pelecanus occidentalis*

___ ___ Black-crowned Night-Heron, *Nycticorax nycticorax*

DATE

. . . .

___ ___ Yellow-crowned Night-Heron(S), *Nycticorax violaceus*

___ ___ White Ibis(S), *Eudocimus albus*

___ ___ Mute Swan(N), *Cygnus olor*

PLACE

. . . .

BIRDS OF PREY

___ ___ Bald Eagle, *Haliaeetus leucocephalus*

___ ___ Sharp-shinned Hawk, *Accipiter striatus*

SPECIES SIGHTED

. . . .

___ ___ Cooper's Hawk, *Accipiter cooperii*

___ ___ Red-tailed Hawk, *Buteo jamaicensis*

NUMBER

___ ___ Rough-legged Hawk(N), *Buteo lagopus*

___ ___ Merlin, *Falco columbarius*

___ ___ Peregrine Falcon, *Falco peregrinus*

GALLINULES

___ ___ Common Moorhen, *Gallinula chloropus*

GULLS

___ ___ Laughing Gull, *Larus atricilla*

___ ___ Bonaparte's Gull, *Larus philadelphia*

___ ___ Ring-billed Gull, *Larus delawarensis*

DOVES

___ ___ Mourning Dove, *Zenaida macroura*

OWLS AND WOODPECKERS

Northern Saw-whet Owl(N), *Aegolius acadicus* ___ ___

Red-headed Woodpecker, *Melanerpes erythrocephalus* ___ ___

Yellow-bellied Sapsucker, *Sphyrapicus varius* ___ ___

SWALLOWS, THRUSHES, AND STARLINGS

Tree Swallow, *Tachycineta bicolor* ___ ___

American Robin, *Turdus migratorius* ___ ___

European Starling, *Sturnus vulgaris* ___ ___

WARBLERS

Yellow-rumped Warbler, *Dendroica coronata* ___ ___

American Redstart, *Setophaga ruticilla* ___ ___

GROSBEAKS AND SPARROWS

Blue Grosbeak, *Guiraca caerulea* ___ ___

Indigo Bunting, *Passerina cyanea* ___ ___

Chipping Sparrow, *Spizella passerina* ___ ___

BLACKBIRDS AND ORIOLES

Red-winged Blackbird, *Agelaius phoeniceus* ___ ___

Orchard Oriole, *Icterus spurius* ___ ___

Northern Oriole, *Icterus galbula* ___ ___

COMMENTS AND SIGHTING NOTES

. . . .

Birds of Prey

SIGHTINGS OF VULTURES, EAGLES, AND HAWKS

Families Cathartidae *and* Accipitridae

♂	♀	JUV.	IMM.	VULTURES
___	___	___	___	Black Vulture (S), *Coragyps atratus*
___	___	___	___	Turkey Vulture, *Cathartes aura*

DATE

. . . .

PLACE

. . . .

SPECIES SIGHTED

. . . .

NUMBER

				EAGLES AND HAWKS
___	___	___	___	Osprey, *Pandion haliaetus*
___	___	___	___	Bald Eagle, *Haliaeetus leucocephalus*
___	___	___	___	Northern Harrier, *Circus cyaneus*
___	___	___	___	Sharp-shinned Hawk, *Accipiter striatus*
___	___	___	___	Cooper's Hawk, *Accipiter cooperii*
___	___	___	___	Red-shouldered Hawk, *Buteo lineatus*
___	___	___	___	Broad-winged Hawk, *Buteo platypterus*
___	___	___	___	Swainson's Hawk (W), *Buteo swainsoni*
___	___	___	___	Red-tailed Hawk, *Buteo jamaicensis*

	♂	♀	JUV.	IMM.
Ferruginous Hawk, *Buteo regalis*	——	——	——	——
Rough-legged Hawk, *Buteo lagopus*	——	——	——	——
Golden Eagle, *Aquila chrysaetos*	——	——	——	——

FALCONS

	♂	♀	JUV.	IMM.
American Kestrel, *Falco sparverius*	——	——	——	——
Merlin, *Falco columbarius*	——	——	——	——
Peregrine Falcon, *Falco peregrinus*	——	——	——	——
Gyrfalcon, *Falco rusticolus*	——	——	——	——

COMMENTS AND SIGHTING NOTES

. . . .

Woodland Birds in Spring Plumages

BEGINNING ON

. . . .

D A T E

AND ENDING ON

. . . .

D A T E

AT

. . . .

P L A C E

SPECIES SIGHTED

(Fill in ♂, ♀, Juv., or Imm.)

HERONS, IBISES, AND SPOONBILLS

_____ Great Blue Heron, *Ardea herodias*

_____ Great Egret, *Casmerodius albus*

_____ Snowy Egret, *Egretta thula*

_____ Little Blue Heron, *Egretta caerulea*

_____ Tricolored Heron, *Egretta tricolor*

_____ Reddish Egret, *Egretta rufescens*

_____ Cattle Egret, *Bubulcus ibis*

_____ Green-backed Heron, *Butorides striatus*

_____ Black-crowned Night-Heron, *Nycticorax nycticorax*

_____ Yellow-crowned Night-Heron, *Nycticorax violaceus*

_____ White Ibis, *Eudocimus albus*

_____ Glossy Ibis, *Plegadis falcinellus*

_____ White-faced Ibis, *Plegadis chihi*

_____ Roseate Spoonbill, *Ajaia ajaja*

DUCKS

_____ Wood Duck, *Aix sponsa*

_____ American Black Duck(N), *Anas rubripes*

_____ Common Goldeneye(N), *Bucephala clangula*

_____ Hooded Merganser, *Lophodytes cucullatus*

VULTURES

_____ Black Vulture(S), *Coragyps atratus*

_____ Turkey Vulture, *Cathartes aura*

KITES, HAWKS, AND FALCONS

American Swallow-tailed Kite, _____
Elanoides forficatus

Sharp-shinned Hawk, _____
Accipiter striatus

Cooper's Hawk, _____
Accipiter cooperii

Northern Goshawk(N), _____
Accipiter gentilis

Red-shouldered Hawk, _____
Buteo lineatus

Broad-winged Hawk, _____
Buteo platypterus

Red-tailed Hawk, _____
Buteo jamaicensis

Merlin(N), _____
Falco columbarius

GROUSE AND TURKEYS

Spruce Grouse(N), _____
Dendragapus canadensis

Ruffed Grouse(N), *Bonasa umbellus* _____

Wild Turkey(S), *Meleagris gallopavo* _____

WOODCOCK

American Woodcock, *Scolopax minor* _____

DOVES AND CUCKOOS

Mourning Dove, *Zenaida macroura* _____

Black-billed Cuckoo, _____
Coccyzus erythropthalmus

Yellow-billed Cuckoo, _____
Coccyzus americanus

OWLS

_____ Eastern Screech-Owl, *Otus asio*

_____ Great Horned Owl, *Bubo virginianus*

_____ Barred Owl, *Strix varia*

_____ Long-eared Owl(N), *Asio otus*

_____ Northern Saw-whet Owl(N), *Aegolius acadicus*

GOATSUCKERS

_____ Chuck-will's-widow(S), *Caprimulgus carolinensis*

_____ Whip-poor-will, *Caprimulgus vociferus*

SWIFTS AND HUMMINGBIRDS

_____ Chimney Swift, *Chaetura pelagica*

_____ Ruby-throated Hummingbird, *Archilochus colubris*

KINGFISHERS, WOODPECKERS, AND ALLIES

_____ Belted Kingfisher, *Ceryle alcyon*

_____ Red-headed Woodpecker, *Melanerpes erythrocephalus*

_____ Red-bellied Woodpecker, *Melanerpes carolinus*

_____ Yellow-bellied Sapsucker, *Sphyrapicus varius*

_____ Downy Woodpecker, *Picoides pubescens*

_____ Hairy Woodpecker, *Picoides villosus*

_____ Red-cockaded Woodpecker(S), *Picoides borealis*

_____ Three-toed Woodpecker(N), *Picoides tridactylus*

_____ Black-backed Woodpecker(N), *Picoides arcticus*

_____ Northern Flicker, *Colaptes auratus*

_____ Pileated Woodpecker, *Dryocopus pileatus*

FLYCATCHERS

Olive-sided Flycatcher, *Mionectes olivaceus* _____

Eastern Wood-Pewee, *Contopus virens* _____

Yellow-bellied Flycatcher(N), *Empidonax flaviventris* _____

Acadian Flycatcher, *Empidonax virescens* _____

Least Flycatcher(N), *Empidonax minimus* _____

Eastern Phoebe, *Sayornis phoebe* _____

Eastern Kingbird, *Tyrannus tyrannus* _____

Gray Kingbird, *Tyrannus dominicensis* _____

SWALLOWS

Tree Swallow(N), *Tachycineta bicolor* _____

Barn Swallow, *Hirundo rustica* _____

JAYS AND CROWS

Gray Jay(N), *Perisoreus canadensis* _____

Blue Jay, *Cyanocitta cristata* _____

Scrub Jay(S), *Aphelocoma coerulescens* _____

American Crow, *Corvus brachyrhynchos* _____

Fish Crow, *Corvus ossifragus* _____

Common Raven(N), *Corvus corax* _____

CHICKADEES

Black-capped Chickadee(N), *Parus atricapillus* _____

Carolina Chickadee(S), *Parus carolinensis* _____

Boreal Chickadee(N), *Parus hudsonicus* _____

NUTHATCHES, CREEPERS, AND WRENS

Red-breasted Nuthatch(N), *Sitta canadensis* _____

Brown-headed Nuthatch, *Sitta pusilla* _____

Brown Creeper, *Certhia americana* _____

Carolina Wren, *Thryothorus ludovicianus* _____

Bewick's Wren, *Thryomanes bewickii* _____

_____ House Wren, *Troglodytes aedon*
_____ Winter Wren (N), *Troglodytes troglodytes*

KINGLETS AND GNATCATCHERS

_____ Golden-crowned Kinglet, *Regulus satrapa*
_____ Ruby-crowned Kinglet, *Regulus calendula*
_____ Blue-gray Gnatcatcher, *Polioptila caerulea*

THRUSHES AND ALLIES

_____ Eastern Bluebird, *Sialia sialis*
_____ Veery (N), *Catharus fuscescens*
_____ Gray-cheeked Thrush (N), *Catharus minimus*
_____ Swainson's Thrush (N), *Catharus ustulatus*
_____ Hermit Thrush (N), *Catharus guttatus*
_____ Wood Thrush, *Hylocichla mustelina*
_____ American Robin, *Turdus migratorius*

MOCKINGBIRDS AND THRASHERS

_____ Gray Catbird, *Dumetella carolinensis*
_____ Northern Mockingbird, *Mimus polyglottos*
_____ Brown Thrasher, *Toxostoma rufum*

WAXWINGS, STARLINGS, AND VIREOS

_____ Cedar Waxwing (N), *Bombycilla cedrorum*
_____ European Starling, *Sturnus vulgaris*
_____ White-eyed Vireo (S), *Vireo griseus*
_____ Bell's Vireo (W), *Vireo bellii*
_____ Solitary Vireo, *Vireo solitarius*
_____ Yellow-throated Vireo, *Vireo flavifrons*
_____ Warbling Vireo, *Vireo gilvus*
_____ Philadelphia Vireo (N), *Vireo philadelphicus*
_____ Red-eyed Vireo, *Vireo olivaceus*

WARBLERS

Blue-winged Warbler, *Vermivora pinus* _____

Golden-winged Warbler (N), *Vermivora* _____
chrysoptera

Tennessee Warbler (N), *Vermivora peregrina* _____

Nashville Warbler (N), *Vermivora ruficapilla* _____

Northern Parula, *Parula americana* _____

Yellow Warbler, *Dendroica petechia* _____

Chestnut-sided Warbler (N), *Dendroica* _____
pensylvanica

Magnolia Warbler (N), *Dendroica magnolia* _____

Cape May Warbler (N), *Dendroica tigrina* _____

Black-throated Blue Warbler (N), *Dendroica* _____
caerulescens

Yellow-rumped Warbler (N), *Dendroica* _____
coronata

Black-throated Green Warbler (N), *Dendroica* _____
virens

Blackburnian Warbler (N), *Dendroica fusca* _____

Yellow-throated Warbler (S), *Dendroica* _____
dominica

Pine Warbler, *Dendroica pinus* _____

Prairie Warbler, *Dendroica discolor* _____

Palm Warbler (N), *Dendroica palmarum* _____

Bay-breasted Warbler (N), *Dendroica castanea* _____

Cerulean Warbler, *Dendroica cerulea* _____

Black-and-white Warbler, *Mniotilta varia* _____

American Redstart, *Setophaga ruticilla* _____

Prothonotary Warbler, *Protonotaria citrea* _____

Worm-eating Warbler, *Helmitheros* _____
vermivorus

Swainson's Warbler (S), *Limnothlypis* _____
swainsonii

Ovenbird, *Seiurus aurocapillus* _____

Northern Waterthrush (N), *Seiurus* _____
noveboracensis

_____ Louisiana Waterthrush, *Seiurus motacilla*

_____ Kentucky Warbler, *Oporornis formosus*

_____ Mourning Warbler(N), *Oporornis philadelphia*

_____ Common Yellowthroat, *Geothlypis trichas*

_____ Hooded Warbler, *Wilsonia citrina*

_____ Wilson's Warbler(N), *Wilsonia pusilla*

_____ Canada Warbler(N), *Wilsonia candensis*

TANAGERS, CARDINALS, AND GROSBEAKS

_____ Summer Tanager(S), *Piranga rubra*

_____ Scarlet Tanager, *Piranga olivacea*

_____ Northern Cardinal, *Cardinalis cardinalis*

_____ Rose-breasted Grosbeak, *Pheucticus ludovicianus*

_____ Blue Grosbeak(S), *Guiraca caerulea*

_____ Indigo Bunting, *Passerina cyanea*

_____ Painted Bunting(S), *Passerina ciris*

TOWHEES, SPARROWS, AND ALLIES

_____ Rufous-sided Towhee, *Pipilo erythrophthalmus*

_____ Bachman's Sparrow(S), *Aimophila aestivalis*

_____ Chipping Sparrow, *Spizella passerina*

Clay-colored Sparrow (NW), *Spizella pallida* _____

Lark Sparrow (W), *Chondestes grammacus* _____

Song Sparrow, *Melospiza melodia* _____

Lincoln's Sparrow (N), *Melospiza lincolnii* _____

Swamp Sparrow, *Melospiza georgiana* _____

White-throated Sparrow, *Zonotrichia albicollis* _____

Dark-eyed Junco (N), *Junco hyemalis* _____

BLACKBIRDS AND ORIOLES

Rusty Blackbird (N), *Euphagus carolinus* _____

Common Grackle, *Quiscalus quiscula* _____

Brown-headed Cowbird, *Molothrus ater* _____

Orchard Oriole, *Icterus spurius* _____

Northern Oriole, *Icterus galbula* _____

FINCHES AND ALLIES

Pine Grosbeak (N), *Pinicola enucleator* _____

Purple Finch (N), *Carpodacus purpureus* _____

House Finch, *Carpodacus mexicanus* _____

Red Crossbill (N), *Loxia curvirostra* _____

White-winged Crossbill (N), *Loxia leucoptera* _____

Pine Siskin (N), *Carduelis pinus* _____

Evening Grosbeak (N), *Coccothraustes verpertinus* _____

The Nightbird Search

BEGINNING AT

. . . .
T   I   M   E

**AND
ENDING AT**

. . . .
T   I   M   E

ON

. . . .
D   A   T   E

AT

. . . .
P   L   A   C   E

SPECIES SIGHTED
(Fill in ♂, ♀, Juv., or Imm.)

_____ Common Barn-Owl, *Tyto alba*

_____ Eastern Screech-Owl, *Otus asio*

_____ Great Horned Owl, *Bubo virginianus*

_____ Barred Owl, *Strix varia*

_____ Great Gray Owl, *Strix nebulosa*

_____ Long-eared Owl, *Asio otus*

_____ Short-eared Owl, *Asio flammeus*

_____ Northern Saw-whet Owl, *Aegolius acadicus*

_____ Common Nighthawk, *Chordeiles minor*

_____ Common Poorwill(W), *Phalaenoptilus nuttallii*

_____ Chuck-will's-widow, *Caprimulgus carolinensis*

_____ Whip-poor-will, *Caprimulgus vociferus*

The 24-Hour Spring Field Birdwatch

DATE

. . . .

PLACE

. . . .

SPECIES SIGHTED

. . . .

NUMBER

SPECIES SIGHTED

♂	♀	JUV.	IMM.	VULTURES
___	___	___	___	Turkey Vulture, *Cathartes aura*

KITES, HAWKS, AND FALCONS

___	___	___	___	Mississippi Kite(S), *Ictinia mississippiensis*
___	___	___	___	Northern Harrier, *Circus cyaneus*
___	___	___	___	Red-tailed Hawk, *Buteo jamaicensis*
___	___	___	___	American Kestrel, *Falco sparverius*

PARTRIDGES, GROUSE, TURKEYS, AND QUAIL

	♂	♀	JUV.	IMM.
Gray Partridge(NW), *Perdix perdix*	—	—	—	—
Ring-necked Pheasant(N), *Phasianus colchicus*	—	—	—	—
Greater Prairie-Chicken(NW), *Tympanuchus cupido*	—	—	—	—
Northern Bobwhite, *Colinus virginianus*	—	—	—	—

SHOREBIRDS

	♂	♀	JUV.	IMM.
Killdeer, *Charadrius vociferus*	—	—	—	—
Upland Sandpiper(N), *Bartramia longicauda*	—	—	—	—
Common Snipe(N), *Gallinago gallinago*	—	—	—	—

♂	♀	JUV.	IMM.	PIGEONS AND DOVES
—	—	—	—	Rock Dove, *Columba livia*
—	—	—	—	Mourning Dove, *Zenaida macroura*
—	—	—	—	Common Ground-Dove(S), *Columbina passerina*

OWLS, GOATSUCKERS, AND SWIFTS

♂	♀	JUV.	IMM.	
—	—	—	—	Common Barn-Owl, *Tyto alba*
—	—	—	—	Short-eared Owl(N), *Asio flammeus*
—	—	—	—	Common Nighthawk, *Chordeiles minor*
—	—	—	—	Chimney Swift, *Chaetura pelagica*

WOODPECKERS

♂	♀	JUV.	IMM.	
—	—	—	—	Northern Flicker, *Colaptes auratus*

FLYCATCHERS

♂	♀	JUV.	IMM.	
—	—	—	—	Alder Flycatcher, *Empidonax alnorum*
—	—	—	—	Willow Flycatcher(N), *Empidonax traillii*
—	—	—	—	Scissor-tailed Flycatcher, *Tyrannus forficatus*

LARKS AND SWALLOWS

♂	♀	JUV.	IMM.	
—	—	—	—	Horned Lark, *Eremophila alpestris*
—	—	—	—	Tree Swallow(N), *Tachycineta bicolor*

	♂	♀	JUV.	IMM.
Northern Rough-winged Swallow, *Stegidopteryx ruficollis*	___	___	___	___
Bank Swallow, *Riparia riparia*	___	___	___	___
Cliff Swallow, *Hirundo pyrrhonota*	___	___	___	___
Barn Swallow, *Hirundo rustica*	___	___	___	___

CROWS AND WRENS

	♂	♀	JUV.	IMM.
American Crow, *Corvus brachyrhynchos*	___	___	___	___
Bewick's Wren, *Thryomanes bewickii*	___	___	___	___
Sedge Wren, *Cistothorus platensis*	___	___	___	___

THRUSHES AND MOCKINGBIRDS

	♂	♀	JUV.	IMM.
American Robin, *Turdus migratorius*	___	___	___	___
Northern Mockingbird, *Mimus polyglottos*	___	___	___	___

SHRIKES AND STARLINGS

	♂	♀	JUV.	IMM.
Loggerhead Shrike, *Lanius ludovicianus*	___	___	___	___
European Starling, *Sturnis vulgarus*	___	___	___	___

WARBLERS

	♂	♀	JUV.	IMM.
Blue-winged Warbler, *Vermivora pinus*	___	___	___	___
Yellow Warbler, *Dendroica petechia*	___	___	___	___
Palm Warbler(N), *Dendroica palmarum*	___	___	___	___

♂	♀	JUV.	IMM.	
___	___	___	___	Common Yellowthroat, *Geothlypis trichas*
___	___	___	___	Yellow-breasted Chat, *Icteria virens*

GROSBEAKS, SPARROWS, AND BUNTINGS

♂	♀	JUV.	IMM.	
___	___	___	___	Indigo Bunting, *Passerina cyanea*
___	___	___	___	Dickcissel (W), *Spiza americana*
___	___	___	___	Chipping Sparrow, *Spizella passerina*
___	___	___	___	Clay-colored Sparrow (NW), *Spizella pallida*
___	___	___	___	Field Sparrow, *Spizella pusilla*
___	___	___	___	Vesper Sparrow, *Pooecetes gramineus*
___	___	___	___	Lark Bunting (NW), *Calamospiza melanocorys*
___	___	___	___	Savannah Sparrow (N), *Passerculus sandwichensis*
___	___	___	___	Grasshopper Sparrow, *Ammodramus savannarum*
___	___	___	___	Henslow's Sparrow (N), *Ammodramus henslowii*
___	___	___	___	LeConte's Sparrow (NW), *Ammodramus leconteii*
___	___	___	___	Sharp-tailed Sparrow (N), *Ammodramus caudacutus*

MEADOWLARKS, BLACKBIRDS, AND ORIOLES	♂	♀	JUV.	IMM.
Bobolink(N), *Dolichonyx oryzivorus*	—	—	—	—
Red-winged Blackbird, *Agelaius phoeniceus*	—	—	—	—
Eastern Meadowlark, *Sturnella magna*	—	—	—	—
Western Meadowlark(W), *Sturnella neglecta*	—	—	—	—
Brewer's Blackbird(NW), *Euphagus cyanocephalus*	—	—	—	—
Boat-tailed Grackle(S), *Quiscalus major*	—	—	—	—
Common Grackle, *Quiscalus quiscula*	—	—	—	—
Brown-headed Cowbird, *Molothrus ater*	—	—	—	—

FINCHES AND ALLIES

	♂	♀	JUV.	IMM.
House Finch, *Carpodacus mexicanus*	—	—	—	—
American Goldfinch(N), *Carduelis tristis*	—	—	—	—
House Sparrow, *Passer domesticus*	—	—	—	—

COMMENTS AND SIGHTING NOTES

. . . .

The Spring Weekend Warbler Watch

Subfamily Parulinae *(by Genus)*

♂	♀	JUV.	IMM.	GENUS *Vermivora*
——	——	——	——	Blue-winged Warbler, *Vermivora pinus*
——	——	——	——	Golden-winged Warbler (N), *Vermivora chrysoptera*
——	——	——	——	Tennessee Warbler (N), *Vermivora peregrina*
——	——	——	——	Nashville Warbler, *Vermivora ruficapilla*
				GENUS *Parula*
——	——	——	——	Northern Parula, *Parula americana*

DATE

. . . .

PLACE

. . . .

SPECIES
SIGHTED

. . . .

NUMBER

GENUS *Dendroica*	♂	♀	JUV.	IMM.
Yellow Warbler, *Dendroica petechia*	___	___	___	___
Chestnut-sided Warbler (N), *Dendroica pensylvanica*	___	___	___	___
Magnolia Warbler, *Dendroica magnolia*	___	___	___	___
Black-throated Blue Warbler (N), *Dendroica caerulescens*	___	___	___	___
Yellow-rumped Warbler (N), *Dendroica coronata*	___	___	___	___
Black-throated Green Warbler (N), *Dendroica virens*	___	___	___	___
Blackburnian Warbler (N), *Dendroica fusca*	___	___	___	___
Yellow-throated Warbler (S), *Dendroica dominica*	___	___	___	___
Pine Warbler, *Dendroica pinus*	___	___	___	___
Prairie Warbler, *Dendroica discolor*	___	___	___	___
Palm Warbler (N), *Dendroica palmarum*	___	___	___	___
Bay-breasted Warbler (N), *Dendroica castanea*	___	___	___	___
Blackpoll Warbler, *Dendroica striata*	___	___	___	___

COMMENTS AND SIGHTING NOTES

. . . .

♂	♀	JUV.	IMM.	GENUS *Mniotilta*
___	___	___	___	Black-and-white Warbler, *Mniotilta varia*
				GENUS *Setophaga*
___	___	___	___	American Redstart, *Setophaga ruticilla*
				GENUS *Protonotaria*
___	___	___	___	Protonotary Warbler, *Protonotaria citrea*
				GENUS *Seiurus*
___	___	___	___	Ovenbird, *Seiurus aurocapillus*
___	___	___	___	Northern Waterthrush, *Seiurus noveboracensis*
___	___	___	___	Louisiana Waterthrush, *Seiurus motacilla*
				GENUS *Oporornis*
___	___	___	___	Kentucky Warbler (S), *Oporornis formosus*
___	___	___	___	Mourning Warbler, *Oporornis philadelphia*

GENUS *Geothlypis*	♂	♀	JUV.	IMM.
Common Yellowthroat, *Geothlypis trichas*	___	___	___	___

GENUS *Wilsonia*

	♂	♀	JUV.	IMM.
Hooded Warbler, *Wilsonia citrina*	___	___	___	___
Wilson's Warbler (N), *Wilsonia pusilla*	___	___	___	___
Canada Warbler (N), *Wilsonia canadensis*	___	___	___	___

GENUS *Icteria*

	♂	♀	JUV.	IMM.
Yellow-breasted Chat, *Icteria virens*	___	___	___	___

Year List of Birds in Flight

♂, ♀, JUV., or IMM.	SPECIES	SIGHTED (DATE)	AT (PLACE)

SPECIES	SIGHTED (DATE)	AT (PLACE)	♂, ♀, JUV., or IMM.

The Fall Weekend Warbler Watch

DATE

. . . .

PLACE

. . . .

SPECIES SIGHTED

. . . .

N U M B E R

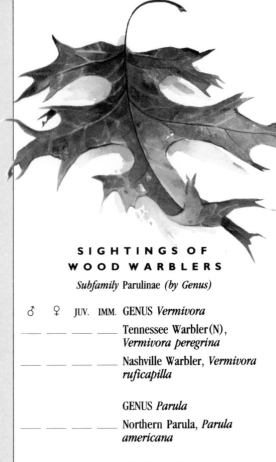

SIGHTINGS OF WOOD WARBLERS

Subfamily Parulinae *(by Genus)*

♂	♀	JUV.	IMM.	GENUS *Vermivora*
—	—	—	—	Tennessee Warbler (N), *Vermivora peregrina*
—	—	—	—	Nashville Warbler, *Vermivora ruficapilla*
				GENUS *Parula*
—	—	—	—	Northern Parula, *Parula americana*
				GENUS *Dendroica*
—	—	—	—	Yellow Warbler, *Dendroica petechia*
—	—	—	—	Chestnut-sided Warbler, *Dendroica pensylvanica*
—	—	—	—	Magnolia Warbler, *Dendroica magnolia*
—	—	—	—	Black-throated Blue Warbler, *Dendroica caerulescens*
—	—	—	—	Yellow-rumped Warbler, *Dendroica coronata*

	♂	♀	JUV.	IMM.
Black-throated Green Warbler, *Dendroica virens*	—	—	—	—
Yellow-throated Warbler, *Dendroica dominica*	—	—	—	—
Pine Warbler, *Dendroica pinus*	—	—	—	—
Prairie Warbler, *Dendroica discolor*	—	—	—	—
Palm Warbler, *Dendroica palmarum*	—	—	—	—
Blackpoll Warbler, *Dendroica striata*	—	—	—	—

GENUS *Mniotilta*

	♂	♀	JUV.	IMM.
Black-and-white Warbler, *Mniotilta varia*	—	—	—	—

GENUS *Setophaga*

	♂	♀	JUV.	IMM.
American Redstart, *Setophaga ruticilla*	—	—	—	—

GENUS *Seiurus*

	♂	♀	JUV.	IMM.
Ovenbird, *Seiurus aurocapillus*	—	—	—	—
Northern Waterthrush, *Seiurus noveboracensis*	—	—	—	—
Louisiana Waterthrush, *Seiurus motacilla*	—	—	—	—

GENUS *Geothlypis*

	♂	♀	JUV.	IMM.
Common Yellowthroat, *Geothlypis trichas*	—	—	—	—

GENUS *Wilsonia*

	♂	♀	JUV.	IMM.
Wilson's Warbler (N), *Wilsonia pusilla*	—	—	—	—
Canada Warbler (N), *Wilsonia canadensis*	—	—	—	—

GENUS *Icteria*

	♂	♀	JUV.	IMM.
Yellow-breasted Chat, *Icteria virens*	—	—	—	—

COMMENTS AND SIGHTING NOTES

. . . .

Wintering Birds

BEGINNING ON

. . . .
D   A   T   E

**AND
ENDING ON**

. . . .
D   A   T   E

AT

. . . .
P   L   A   C   E

SPECIES SIGHTED

(Fill in ♂, ♀)

LOONS, GREBES, AND CORMORANTS

___ Red-throated Loon(N), *Gavia stellata*

___ Common Loon(N), *Gavia immer*

___ Horned Grebe, *Podiceps auritus*

___ Red-necked Grebe, *Podiceps grisegena*

___ Great Cormorant(N), *Phalacrocorax carbo*

HERONS AND IBISES

___ Great Blue Heron, *Ardea herodias*

___ Great Egret(S), *Casmerodius albus*

___ Snowy Egret(S), *Egretta thula*

___ Black-crowned Night-Heron(S), *Nycticorax nycticorax*

___ Glossy Ibis(S), *Plegadis falcinellus*

GEESE AND DUCKS

___ Tundra Swan, *Cygnus columbianus*

___ Snow Goose(S), *Chen caerulescens*

___ Brant, *Branta bernicla*

___ Common Eider, *Somateria mollissima*

___ Harlequin Duck(N), *Histrionicus histrionicus*

___ Oldsquaw(N), *Clangula hyemalis*

___ Black Scoter, *Melanitta nigra*

Surf Scoter, *Melanitta perspicillata* ___
White-winged Scoter, *Melanitta fusca* ___
Common Goldeneye, *Bucephala clangula* ___
Barrow's Goldeneye(N), *Bucephala islandica* ___
Red-breasted Merganser, *Mergus serrator* ___

H A W K S
Rough-legged Hawk, *Buteo lagopus* ___

R A I L S
Virginia Rail(S), *Rallus limicola* ___
Sora(S), *Porzana carolina* ___

PLOVERS AND OYSTERCATCHERS

___ Black-bellied Plover, *Pluvialis squatarola*

___ Wilson's Plover(SE), *Charadrius wilsonia*

___ Piping Plover, *Charadrius melodus*

___ Killdeer, *Charadrius vociferus*

___ American Oystercatcher, *Haematopus palliatus*

SANDPIPERS AND ALLIES

___ Greater Yellowlegs(S), *Tringa melanoleuca*

___ Lesser Yellowlegs(S), *Tringa flavipes*

___ Willet(S), *Catoptrophorus semipalmatus*

___ Spotted Sandpiper(S), *Actitis macularia*

___ Marbled Godwit(S), *Limosa fedoa*

___ Ruddy Turnstone, *Arenaria interpres*

___ Red Knot, *Calidris canutus*

___ Semipalmated Sandpiper(S), *Calidris pusilla*

___ Western Sandpiper(S), *Calidris mauri*

___ Least Sandpiper(S), *Calidris minutilla*

___ Purple Sandpiper(N,S), *Calidris maritima*

___ Dunlin(N,S), *Calidris alpina*

___ Common Snipe, *Gallinago gallinago*

___ American Woodcock(S), *Scolopax minor*

GULLS AND TERNS

___ Laughing Gull(S), *Larus atricilla*

___ Ring-billed Gull, *Larus delawarensis*

___ Herring Gull, *Larus argentatus*

___ Iceland Gull(N), *Larus glaucoides*

___ Great Black-backed Gull, *Larus marinus*

Royal Tern(S), *Sterna maxima* ___

Common Tern(S), *Sterna hirundo* ___

Forster's Tern(S), *Sterna forsteri* ___

Black Skimmer(S), *Rynchops niger* ___

PIGEONS AND DOVES

Rock Dove, *Columba livia* ___

Mourning Dove, *Zenaida macroura* ___

OWLS

Common Barn-Owl, *Tyto alba* ___

Eastern Screech-Owl, *Otus asio* ___

Great Horned Owl, *Bubo virginianus* ___

Barred Owl, *Strix varia* ___

Long-eared Owl, *Asio otus* ___

Short-eared Owl, *Asio flammeus* ___

Northern Saw-whet Owl, *Aegolius acadicus* ___

KINGFISHERS, WOODPECKERS, AND ALLIES

Belted Kingfisher, *Ceryle alcyon* ___

Red-headed Woodpecker(S), *Melanerpes erythrocephalus* ___

Red-bellied Woodpecker, *Melanerpes carolinus* ___

Yellow-bellied Sapsucker, *Sphyrapicus varius* ___

Downy Woodpecker, *Picoides pubescens* ___

Hairy Woodpecker, *Picoides villosus* ___

Red-cockaded Woodpecker(S), *Picoides borealis* ___

Northern Flicker, *Colaptes auratus* ___

Pileated Woodpecker, *Dryocopus pileatus* ___

FLYCATCHERS, LARKS, AND SWALLOWS

___ Eastern Phoebe(S), *Sayornis phoebe*
___ Horned Lark, *Eremophila alpestris*
___ Tree Swallow(S), *Tachycineta bicolor*

JAYS AND CROWS

___ Blue Jay, *Cyanocitta cristata*
___ American Crow, *Corvus brachyrhynchos*
___ Fish Crow(S), *Corvus ossifragus*

CHICKADEES AND TITMICE

___ Black-capped Chickadee, *Parus atricapillus*
___ Carolina Chickadee(S), *Parus carolinensis*

NUTHATCHES

___ Red-breasted Nuthatch, *Sitta canadensis*
___ White-breasted Nuthatch, *Sitta carolinensis*
___ Brown-headed Nuthatch(S), *Sitta pusilla*

CREEPERS AND WRENS

___ Brown Creeper, *Certhia americana*
___ Carolina Wren, *Thryothorus ludovicianus*
___ Bewick's Wren, *Thryomanes bewickii*
___ House Wren(S), *Troglodytes aedon*
___ Winter Wren, *Troglodytes troglodytes*
___ Sedge Wren, *Cistothorus platensis*
___ Marsh Wren(S), *Cistothorus palustris*

KINGLETS AND GNATCATCHERS

Golden-crowned Kinglet, *Regulus satrapa* ___
Ruby-crowned Kinglet(S), *Regulus calendula* ___
Blue-gray Gnatcatcher(S), *Polioptila caerulea* ___

THRUSHES

Eastern Bluebird, *Sialia sialis* ___
Hermit Thrush, *Catharus guttatus* ___
American Robin, *Turdus migratorius* ___

MOCKINGBIRDS AND PIPITS

Gray Catbird(S), *Dumetella carolinensis* ___
Northern Mockingbird, *Mimus polyglottos* ___
Water Pipit, *Anthus spinoletta* ___

WAXWINGS, SHRIKES, STARLINGS, AND VIREOS

Cedar Waxwing, *Bombycilla cedrorum* ___
Northern Shrike(N), *Lanius excubitor* ___
Loggerhead Shrike(S), *Lanius ludovicianus* ___
European Starling, *Sturnus vulgaris* ___
Solitary Vireo(S), *Vireo solitarius* ___

WARBLERS

Orange-crowned Warbler, *Vermivora celata* ___
Yellow-rumped Warbler(N), *Dendroica coronata* ___
Yellow-throated Warbler(S), *Dendroica dominica* ___
Ovenbird(S), *Seiurus aurocapillus* ___
Common Yellowthroat(S), *Geothlypis trichas* ___

TOWHEES, SPARROWS, AND ALLIES

___ Rufous-sided Towhee, *Pipilo erythrophthalmus*

___ Bachman's Sparrow(S), *Aimophila aestivalis*

___ American Tree Sparrow, *Spizella arborea*

___ Chipping Sparrow(S), *Spizella passerina*

___ Field Sparrow, *Spizella pusilla*

___ Lark Sparrow(S), *Chondestes grammacus*

___ Savannah Sparrow, *Passerculus sandwichensis*

___ Grasshopper Sparrow(S), *Ammodramus savannarum*

___ Henslow's Sparrow(S), *Ammodramus henslowii*

___ LeConte's Sparrow(S), *Ammodramus leconteii*

___ Sharp-tailed Sparrow, *Ammodramus caudacutus*

___ Seaside Sparrow, *Ammodramus maritimus*

___ Song Sparrow, *Melospiza melodia*

___ Lincoln's Sparrow(S), *Melospiza lincolnii*

___ Swamp Sparrow, *Melospiza georgiana*

___ White-throated Sparrow, *Zonotrichia albicollis*

___ White-crowned Sparrow(S), *Zonotrichia leucophrys*

___ Harris' Sparrow(W), *Zonotrichia querula*

___ Dark-eyed Junco, *Junco hyemalis*

___ Lapland Longspur, *Calcarius lapponicus*

___ Smith's Longspur, *Calcarius pictus*

___ Chestnut-collared Longspur, *Calcarius ornatus*

___ Snow Bunting, *Plectrophenax nivalis*

MEADOWLARKS, BLACKBIRDS, AND ORIOLES

Red-winged Blackbird, *Agelaius phoeniceus* ___

Eastern Meadowlark, *Sturnella magna* ___

Western Meadowlark, *Sturnella neglecta* ___

Rusty Blackbird, *Euphagus carolinus* ___

Brewer's Blackbird(S), *Euphagus cyanocephalus* ___

Common Grackle, *Quiscalus quiscula* ___

Brown-headed Cowbird, *Molothrus ater* ___

Northern Oriole(S), *Icterus galbula* ___

FINCHES AND ALLIES

Pine Grosbeak(N), *Pinicola enucleator* ___

Purple Finch(N), *Carpodacus purpureus* ___

House Finch, *Carpodacus mexicanus* ___

Red Crossbill(N), *Loxia curvirostra* ___

Common Redpoll, *Carduelis flammea* ___

Pine Siskin(N), *Carduelis pinus* ___

American Goldfinch, *Carduelis tristis* ___

Evening Grosbeak, *Coccothraustes verpertinus* ___

Canadian Border and Mountain Birds

DATE

. . . .

PLACE

. . . .

SPECIES SIGHTED

. . . .

NUMBER

SPECIES SIGHTED

♂ ♀ JUV. IMM. H A W K S

___ ___ ___ ___ Northern Goshawk, *Accipiter gentilis*

G R O U S E

___ ___ ___ ___ Spruce Grouse, *Dendragapus canadensis*

P U F F I N S

___ ___ ___ ___ Atlantic Puffin, *Fratercula arctica*

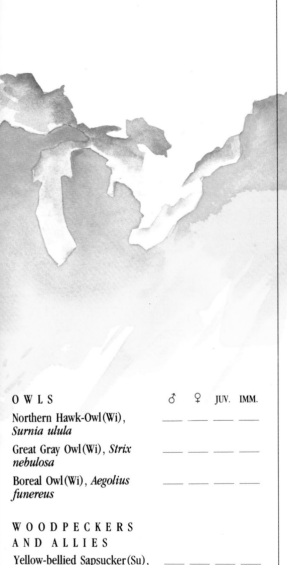

O W L S	♂	♀	JUV.	IMM.
Northern Hawk-Owl(Wi), *Surnia ulula*	___	___	___	___
Great Gray Owl(Wi), *Strix nebulosa*	___	___	___	___
Boreal Owl(Wi), *Aegolius funereus*	___	___	___	___

W O O D P E C K E R S A N D A L L I E S

Yellow-bellied Sapsucker(Su), *Sphyrapicus varius*	___	___	___	___
Three-toed Woodpecker, *Picoides tridactylus*	___	___	___	___
Black-backed Woodpecker, *Picoides arcticus*	___	___	___	___

♂	♀	JUV.	IMM.	FLYCATCHERS
___	___	___	___	Olive-sided Flycatcher(Su), *Mionectes olivaceus*
___	___	___	___	Yellow-bellied Flycatcher(Su), *Empidonax flaviventris*

JAYS AND CROWS

___	___	___	___	Gray Jay, *Perisoreus canadensis*
___	___	___	___	Common Raven, *Corvus corax*

CHICKADEES AND WRENS

___	___	___	___	Boreal Chickadee, *Parus hudsonicus*
___	___	___	___	Winter Wren(Su), *Troglodytes troglodytes*

KINGLETS AND THRUSHES

___	___	___	___	Golden-crowned Kinglet(Su), *Regulus satrapa*
___	___	___	___	Ruby-crowned Kinglet(Su), *Regulus calendula*
___	___	___	___	Gray-cheeked Thrush(Su), *Catharus minimus*
___	___	___	___	Swainson's Thrush(Su), *Catharus ustulatus*
___	___	___	___	Hermit Thrush, *Catharus guttatus*

VIREOS

___	___	___	___	Solitary Vireo(Su), *Vireo solitarius*
___	___	___	___	Philadelphia Vireo(Su), *Vireo philadelphicus*

WARBLERS	♂	♀	JUV.	IMM.
Tennessee Warbler (Su), *Vermivora peregrina*				
Nashville Warbler (Su), *Vermivora ruficapilla*				
Magnolia Warbler (Su), *Dendroica magnolia*				
Cape May Warbler (Su), *Dendroica tigrina*				
Yellow-rumped Warbler (Su), *Dendroica coronata*				
Blackburnian Warbler (Su), *Dendroica fusca*				
Bay-breasted Warbler (Su), *Dendroica castanea*				
Blackpoll Warbler (Su), *Dendroica striata*				
Northern Waterthrush (Su), *Seiurus noveboracensis*				
Mourning Warbler (Su), *Oporonis philadelphia*				
Wilson's Warbler (Su), *Wilsonia pusilla*				
Canada Warbler (Su), *Wilsonia canadensis*				

SPARROWS AND ALLIES

	♂	♀	JUV.	IMM.
LeConte's Sparrow (Su), *Ammodramus leconteii*				
Lincoln's Sparrow (Su), *Melospiza lincolnii*				
White-throated Sparrow (Su), *Zonotrichia albicollis*				
Dark-eyed Junco, *Junco hyemalis*				

Permanent Residents

BEGINNING ON

. . . .

D   A   T   E

**AND
ENDING ON**

. . . .

D   A   T   E

FOR

. . . .

Y   E   A   R

AT

. . . .

P   L   A   C   E

S P E C I E S   S I G H T E D

(Fill in ♂, ♀, Juv., or Imm.)

P E L I C A N S   A N D   D A R T E R S

_____ Brown Pelican (SE), *Pelecanus occidentalis*

_____ Anhinga (S), *Anhinga anhinga*

H E R O N S ,   I B I S E S ,
A N D   S T O R K S

_____ Great Blue Heron, *Ardea herodias*

_____ Tricolored Heron (SE), *Egretta tricolor*

_____ Yellow-crowned Night Heron (S), *Nycticorax violaceus*

_____ White Ibis (SE), *Eudocimus albus*

_____ Wood Stork (SE), *Mycteria americana*

S W A N S ,   G E E S E ,
A N D   D U C K S

_____ Mute Swan (N), *Cygnus olor*

_____ Canada Goose (N), *Branta canadensis*

_____ American Black Duck (N), *Anas rubripes*

_____ Mallard, *Anas platyrhynchos*

KITES AND HAWKS

Swallow-tailed Kite(SE), *Elanoides forficatus* _____

Red-tailed Hawk, *Buteo jamaicensis* _____

American Kestrel, *Falco sparverius* _____

PARTRIDGES, GROUSE, TURKEYS, AND QUAIL

Gray Partridge(NW), *Perdix perdix* _____

Ring-necked Pheasant(N), *Phasianus colchicus* _____

Spruce Grouse(N), *Dendragapus canadensis* _____

Ruffed Grouse(N), *Bonasa umbellus* _____

Greater Prairie-Chicken(NW), *Tympanuchus cupido* _____

Wild Turkey(S), *Meleagris gallopavo* _____

Northern Bobwhite, *Colinus virginianus* _____

RAILS, GALLINULES, AND LIMPKINS

Clapper Rail, *Rallus longirostris* _____

Purple Gallinule(S), *Porphyrula martinica* _____

Limpkin(S), *Aramus guarauna* _____

PLOVERS AND GULLS

Killdeer, *Charadrius vociferus* _____

American Oystercatcher, *Haematopus palliatus* _____

Great Black-backed Gull(N), *Larus marinus* _____

PIGEONS AND DOVES

Rock Dove, *Columba livia* _____

Mourning Dove, *Zenaida macroura* _____

Common Ground-Dove(S), *Columbina passerina* _____

O W L S

_____ Eastern Screech-Owl, *Otus asio*

_____ Great Horned Owl, *Bubo virginianus*

_____ Barred Owl, *Strix varia*

_____ Long-eared Owl(N), *Asio otus*

_____ Short-eared Owl(N), *Asio flammeus*

_____ Northern Saw-whet Owl(N), *Aegolius acadicus*

W O O D P E C K E R S

_____ Red-bellied Woodpecker, *Melanerpes carolinus*

_____ Downy Woodpecker, *Picoides pubescens*

_____ Hairy Woodpecker, *Picoides villosus*

_____ Red-cockaded Woodpecker(S), *Picoides borealis*

_____ Three-toed Woodpecker(N), *Picoides tridactylus*

_____ Black-backed Woodpecker(N), *Picoides arcticus*

_____ Pileated Woodpecker, *Dryocopus pileatus*

J A Y S   A N D   C R O W S

_____ Gray Jay(N), *Perisoreus canadensis*

_____ Blue Jay, *Cyanocitta cristata*

_____ Scrub Jay(S), *Aphelocoma coerulescens*

_____ American Crow, *Corvus brachyrhynchos*

_____ Fish Crow, *Corvus ossifragus*

_____ Common Raven(N), *Corvus corax*

C H I C K A D E E S

_____ Black-capped Chickadee(N), *Parus atricapillus*

_____ Carolina Chickadee(S), *Parus carolinensis*

_____ Boreal Chickadee(N), *Parus hudsonicus*

NUTHATCHES, CREEPERS, AND WRENS

Brown-headed Nuthatch, *Sitta pusilla* _____
Brown Creeper, *Certhia americana* _____
Carolina Wren, *Thryothorus ludovicianus* _____
House Wren, *Troglodytes aedon* _____

MOCKINGBIRDS

Northern Mockingbird, *Mimus polyglottos* _____

STARLINGS

European Starling, *Sturnus vulgarus* _____

CARDINALS

Northern Cardinal, *Cardinalis cardinalis* _____

SPARROWS

Song Sparrow, *Melospiza melodia* _____

BLACKBIRDS

Red-winged Blackbird, *Agelaius phoeniceus* _____

FINCHES AND ALLIES

House Finch, *Carpodacus mexicanus* _____
House Sparrow,
Passer domesticus _____

COMMENTS AND SIGHTING NOTES

. . . .

Florida
Specialties

DATE

. . . .

PLACE

. . . .

**SPECIES
SIGHTED**

. . . .

NUMBER

SPECIES SIGHTED

(Fill in ♂, ♀, Juv., or Imm.)

RESIDENTS

Great Blue Heron (White Phase), *Ardea herodias* _____

Greater Flamingo, *Phoenicopterus ruber* _____

Snail Kite, *Rostrhamus sociabilis* _____

Short-tailed Hawk, *Buteo brachyurus* _____

Crested Caracara, *Polyborus plancus* _____

White-crowned Pigeon, *Columba leucocephala* _____

Mangrove Cuckoo, *Coccyzus minor* _____

Groove-billed Ani, *Crotophaga sulcirostris* _____

Burrowing Owl, *Athene cunicularia* _____

Black-whiskered Vireo, *Vireo altiloquus* _____

Scrub Jay, *Aphelocoma coerulescens* _____

INTRODUCED SPECIES

Canary-winged Parakeet, *Brotogeris versicolurus* _____

Red-whiskered Bulbul, *Pycnonotus jocosus* _____

Spot-breasted Oriole, *Icterus pectoralis* _____

Vagrant
Species

COMMENTS	SPECIES	SIGHTED (DATE)	AT (PLACE)

SPECIES	SIGHTED (DATE)	AT (PLACE)	COMMENTS

Arctic and Alpine Birds

DATE

. . . .

PLACE

. . . .

SPECIES SIGHTED

. . . .

N U M B E R

SPECIES SIGHTED

♂ ♀ JUV. IMM.

___ ___ ___ ___ Common Loon, *Gavia immer*

___ ___ ___ ___ Arctic Loon, *Gavia arctica*

___ ___ ___ ___ Tundra Swan, *Cygnus columbianus*

___ ___ ___ ___ King Eider (N), *Somateria spectabilis*

___ ___ ___ ___ Rough-legged Hawk, *Buteo lagopus*

___ ___ ___ ___ Gyrfalcon (N), *Falco rusticolis*

___ ___ ___ ___ Glaucous Gull, *Larus hyperboreus*

	♂	♀	JUV.	IMM.
Snowy Owl(N), *Nyctea scandiaca*	___	___	___	___
Water Pipit, *Anthus spinoletta*	___	___	___	___
Northern Shrike, *Lanius excubitor*	___	___	___	___
Lapland Longspur, *Calcarius lapponicus*	___	___	___	___
Snow Bunting, *Plectrophenax nivalis*	___	___	___	___
Common Redpoll, *Carduelis flammea*	___	___	___	___

North American Travel List

SPECIES	SIGHTED (DATE)	AT (PLACE)

SPECIES	SIGHTED (DATE)	AT (PLACE)	COMMENTS AND SIGHTING NOTES
			. . . .

World Travel List

SPECIES	SIGHTED (DATE)	AT (PLACE)

SPECIES	SIGHTED (DATE)	AT (PLACE)

COMMENTS
AND
SIGHTING
NOTES

. . . .

The
Life
List

♂ ♀ Juv. Imm.

LOONS

Red-throated Loon,
Gavia stellata

Arctic Loon, *Gavia
arctica*

Common Loon,
Gavia immer

GREBES

Pied-billed Grebe,
*Podilymbus
podiceps*

Horned Grebe,
Podiceps auritus

Red-necked Grebe,
Podiceps grisegena

Eared Grebe,
Podiceps nigricollis

Western Grebe,
*Aechmophorus
occidentalis*

SHEARWATERS, PETRELS, GANNETS, AND PELICANS

Northern Fulmar,
Fulmarus glacialis

♂ ♀ Juv. Imm.

Cory's Shearwater,
*Calonectris
diomedea*

Greater Shearwater,
Puffinus gravis

Sooty Shearwater,
Puffinus griseus

Manx Shearwater,
Puffinus puffinus

Audubon's
Shearwater,
*Puffinus
lherminieri*

Wilson's Storm-
Petrel, *Oceanites
oceanicus*

Leach's Storm-
Petrel,
*Oceanodroma
leucorhoa*

Northern Gannet,
Sula bassanus

American White
Pelican, *Pelecanus
erythrorhynchos*

Brown Pelican,
*Pelecanus
occidentalis*

CORMORANTS, DARTERS, AND FRIGATEBIRDS

♂ ♀ Juv. Imm.

Great Cormorant, _____ _ _ _
Phalacrocorax carbo

Double-crested _____ _ _ _
Cormorant, *Phalacrocorax auritus*

Olivaceous _____ _ _ _
Cormorant, *Phalacrocorax olivaceus*

Anhinga, *Anhinga* _____ _ _ _
anhinga

Magnificent _____ _ _ _
Frigatebird, *Fregata magnificens*

BITTERNS AND HERONS

American Bittern, _____ _ _ _
Botaurus lentiginosus

Least Bittern, _____ _ _ _
Ixobrychus exilis

Great Blue Heron, _____ _ _ _
Ardea herodias

Great Egret, _____ _ _ _
Casmerodius albus

Snowy Egret, _____ _ _ _
Egretta thula

Little Blue Heron, _____ _ _ _
Egretta caerulea

Tricolored Heron, _____ _ _ _
Egretta tricolor

Reddish Egret, _____ _ _ _
Egretta rufescens

Cattle Egret, _____ _ _ _
Bubulcus ibis

♂ ♀ Juv. Imm.

Green-backed _____ _ _ _
Heron, *Butorides striatus*

Black-crowned _____ _ _ _
Night-Heron, *Nycticorax nycticorax*

Yellow-crowned _____ _ _ _
Night-Heron, *Nycticorax violaceus*

IBISES, SPOONBILLS, STORKS, AND FLAMINGOS

White Ibis, _____ _ _ _
Eudocimus albus

Glossy Ibis, _____ _ _ _
Plegadis falcinellus

White-faced Ibis, _____ _ _ _
Plegadis chihi

Roseate Spoonbill, _____ _ _ _
Ajaia ajaja

Wood Stork, _____ _ _ _
Mycteria americana

Greater Flamingo, _____ _ _ _
Phoenicopterus ruber

SWANS, GEESE, AND DUCKS

Fulvous Whistling- _____ _ _ _
Duck, *Dendroygna bicolor*

Tundra Swan, _____ _ _ _
Cygnus columbianus

Mute Swan, *Cygnus* _____ _ _ _
olor

♂	♀	Juv.	Imm.	
				Lesser White-fronted Goose, *Anser erythropus*
—	—	—	—	Greater White-fronted Goose, *Anser albifrons*
—	—	—	—	Snow Goose, *Chen caerulescens*
—	—	—	—	Brant, *Branta bernicla*
—	—	—	—	Canada Goose, *Branta canadensis*
—	—	—	—	Wood Duck, *Aix sponsa*
—	—	—	—	Green-winged Teal, *Anas crecca*
—	—	—	—	American Black Duck, *Anas rubripes*
—	—	—	—	Mallard, *Anas platyrhynchos*
—	—	—	—	Northern Pintail, *Anas acuta*
—	—	—	—	Blue-winged Teal, *Anas discors*
—	—	—	—	Northern Shoveler, *Anas clypeata*
—	—	—	—	Gadwall, *Anas strepera*
—	—	—	—	Eurasian Wigeon, *Anas penelope*
—	—	—	—	American Wigeon, *Anas americana*
—	—	—	—	Canvasback, *Aythya valisineria*
—	—	—	—	Redhead, *Aythya americana*
—	—	—	—	Ring-necked Duck, *Aythya collaris*

♂	♀	Juv.	Imm.	
—	—	—	—	Greater Scaup, *Aythya marila*
—	—	—	—	Lesser Scaup, *Aythya affinis*
—	—	—	—	Common Eider, *Somateria mollissima*
—	—	—	—	King Eider, *Somateria spectabilis*
—	—	—	—	Harlequin Duck, *Histrionicus histrionicus*
—	—	—	—	Oldsquaw, *Clangula hyemalis*
—	—	—	—	Black Scoter, *Melanitta nigra*
—	—	—	—	Surf Scoter, *Melanitta perspicillata*
—	—	—	—	White-winged Scoter, *Melanitta fusca*
—	—	—	—	Common Goldeneye, *Bucephala clangula*
—	—	—	—	Barrow's Goldeneye, *Bucephala islandica*
—	—	—	—	Bufflehead, *Bucephala albeola*
—	—	—	—	Hooded Merganser, *Lophodytes cucullatus*
—	—	—	—	Common Merganser, *Mergus merganser*
—	—	—	—	Red-breasted Merganser, *Mergus serrator*

	♂	♀	Juv.	Imm.

Ruddy Duck,
Oxyura jamaicensis — — — —

VULTURES

Black Vulture,
Coragyps atratus — — — —

Turkey Vulture,
Cathartes aura — — — —

KITES, EAGLES, HAWKS, AND ALLIES

Osprey, *Pandion haliaetus* — — — —

American Swallow-tailed Kite,
Elanoides forficatus — — — —

Snail Kite,
Rostrhamus sociabilis — — — —

Mississippi Kite,
Ictinia mississippiensis — — — —

Bald Eagle,
Haliaeetus leucocephalus — — — —

Northern Harrier,
Circus cyaneus — — — —

Sharp-shinned Hawk, *Accipiter striatus* — — — —

Cooper's Hawk,
Accipiter cooperii — — — —

Northern Goshawk,
Accipiter gentilis — — — —

Red-shouldered Hawk, *Buteo lineatus* — — — —

Broad-winged Hawk, *Buteo platypterus* — — — —

Short-tailed Hawk,
Buteo brachyurus — — — —

Swainson's Hawk,
Buteo swainsoni — — — —

Red-tailed Hawk,
Buteo jamaicensis — — — —

Ferruginous Hawk,
Buteo regalis — — — —

Rough-legged Hawk, *Buteo lagopus* — — — —

Golden Eagle,
Aquila chrysaetos — — — —

CARACARAS AND FALCONS

Crested Caracara,
Polyborus plancus — — — —

American Kestrel,
Falco sparverius — — — —

Merlin, *Falco columbarius* — — — —

Peregrine Falcon,
Falco peregrinus — — — —

Gyrfalcon, *Falco rusticolus* — — — —

PARTRIDGES, GROUSE, TURKEYS, AND QUAIL

Gray Partridge,
Perdix perdix — — — —

Ring-necked Pheasant,
Phasianus colchicus — — — —

♂	♀	Juv.	Imm.	
				Spruce Grouse, *Dendragapus canadensis*
_	_	_	_	Willow Ptarmigan, *Lagopus lagopus*
_	_	_	_	Rock Ptarmigan, *Lagopus mutus*
_	_	_	_	Ruffed Grouse, *Bonasa umbellus*
_	_	_	_	Greater Prairie-Chicken, *Tympanuchus cupido*
_	_	_	_	Lesser Prairie-Chicken, *Tympanuchus pallidicinctus*
_	_	_	_	Sharp-tailed Grouse, *Tympanuchus phasianellus*
				Wild Turkey, *Meleagris gallopavo*
_	_	_	_	Northern Bobwhite, *Colinus virginianus*

RAILS, GALLINULES, COOTS, AND LIMPKINS

♂	♀	Juv.	Imm.	
_	_	_	_	Yellow Rail, *Coturnicops noveboracensis*
_	_	_	_	Black Rail, *Laterallus jamaicensis*
_	_	_	_	Clapper Rail, *Rallus longirostris*
_	_	_	_	King Rail, *Rallus elegans*

♂	♀	Juv.	Imm.	
_	_	_	_	Virginia Rail, *Rallus limicola*
_	_	_	_	Sora, *Porzana carolina*
_	_	_	_	Purple Gallinule, *Porphyrula martinica*
_	_	_	_	Common Moorhen, *Gallinula chloropus*
_	_	_	_	American Coot, *Fulica americana*
_	_	_	_	Limpkin, *Aramus guarauna*

CRANES, PLOVERS, AND OYSTERCATCHERS

♂	♀	Juv.	Imm.	
_	_	_	_	Sandhill Crane, *Grus canadensis*
_	_	_	_	Whooping Crane, *Grus americana*
_	_	_	_	Black-bellied Plover, *Pluvialis squatarola*
_	_	_	_	Lesser Golden-Plover, *Pluvialis apricaria*
_	_	_	_	Wilson's Plover, *Charadrius wilsonia*
_	_	_	_	Semipalmated Plover, *Charadrius semipalmatus*
_	_	_	_	Piping Plover, *Charadrius melodus*
_	_	_	_	Killdeer, *Charadrius vociferus*

	♂	♀	Juv.	Imm.

American Oystercatcher, *Haematopus palliatus*

STILTS, AVOCETS, SANDPIPERS, PHALAROPES, AND ALLIES

Black-necked Stilt, *Himantopus mexicanus* — — — —

American Avocet, *Recurvirostra americana* — — — —

Greater Yellowlegs, *Tringa melanoleuca* — — — —

Lesser Yellowlegs, *Tringa flavipes* — — — —

Solitary Sandpiper, *Tringa solitaria* — — — —

Willet, *Catoptrophorus semipalmatus* — — — —

Spotted Sandpiper, *Actitis macularia* — — — —

Upland Sandpiper, *Bartramia longicauda* — — — —

Whimbrel, *Numenius phaeopus* — — — —

Long-billed Curlew, *Numenius americanus* — — — —

Hudsonian Godwit, *Limosa haemastica* — — — —

Marbled Godwit, *Limosa fedoa* — — — —

Ruddy Turnstone, *Arenaria interpres* — — — —

Red Knot, *Calidris canutus* — — — —

Sanderling, *Calidris alba* — — — —

Semipalmated Sandpiper, *Calidris pusilla* — — — —

Western Sandpiper, *Calidris mauri* — — — —

Least Sandpiper, *Calidris minutilla* — — — —

White-rumped Sandpiper, *Calidris fuscicollis* — — — —

Baird's Sandpiper, *Calidris bairdii* — — — —

Pectoral Sandpiper, *Calidris melanotos* — — — —

Purple Sandpiper, *Calidris maritima* — — — —

Dunlin, *Calidris alpina* — — — —

Curlew Sandpiper, *Calidris ferruginea* — — — —

Stilt Sandpiper, *Calidris himantopus* — — — —

Buff-breasted Sandpiper, *Tryngites subruficollis* — — — —

Short-billed Dowitcher, *Limnodromus griseus* — — — —

Long-billed Dowitcher, *Limnodromus scolopaceus* — — — —

_____ Common Snipe,
Gallinago gallinago

_____ American
Woodcock,
Scolopax minor

_____ Wilson's Phalarope,
Phalaropus tricolor

_____ Red-necked
Phalarope,
Phalaropus lobatus

_____ Red Phalarope,
*Phalaropus
fulicaria*

S K U A S ,   G U L L S ,
T E R N S ,   A N D
S K I M M E R S

_____ Pomarine Jaeger,
*Stercorarius
pomarinus*

_____ Parasitic Jaeger,
*Stercorarius
parasiticus*

_____ Long-tailed Jaeger,
*Stercorarius
longicaudus*

_____ Laughing Gull,
Larus artricilla

_____ Franklin's Gull,
Larus pipixcan

_____ Little Gull, *Larus
minutus*

_____ Common Black-
headed Gull, *Larus
ridibundus*

_____ Bonaparte's Gull,
Larus philadelphia

_____ Ring-billed Gull,
Larus delawarensis

_____ Herring Gull, *Larus
argentatus*

_____ Thayer's Gull, *Larus
thayeri*

_____ Iceland Gull, *Larus
glaucoides*

_____ Lesser Black-
backed Gull, *Larus
fuscus*

_____ Glaucous Gull,
Larus hyperboreus

_____ Great Black-backed
Gull, *Larus
marinus*

_____ Black-legged
Kittiwake, *Rissa
tridactyla*

_____ Sabine's Gull, *Xema
sabini*

_____ Ivory Gull,
Pagophila eburnea

_____ Gull-billed Tern,
Sterna nilotica

_____ Caspian Tern,
Sterna caspia

_____ Royal Tern, *Sterna
maxima*

_____ Sandwich Tern,
*Sterna
sandvicensis*

_____ Roseate Tern,
Sterna dougallii

_____ Common Tern,
Sterna hirundo

_____ Arctic Tern, *Sterna
paradisaea*

_____ Forster's Tern,
Sterna forsteri

_____ Least Tern, *Sterna
antillarum*

_____ Black Tern,
Chlidonias niger

	♂	♀	Juv.	Imm.

Black Skimmer, *Rynchops niger* ____ ____ ____ ____

AUKS, MURRES, AND PUFFINS

Dovekie, *Alle alle* ____ ____ ____ ____

Common Murre, *Uria aalge* ____ ____ ____ ____

Thick-billed Murre, *Uria lomvia* ____ ____ ____ ____

Razorbill, *Alca torda* ____ ____ ____ ____

Black Guillemot, *Cepphus grylle* ____ ____ ____ ____

Atlantic Puffin, *Fratercula arctica* ____ ____ ____ ____

PIGEONS AND DOVES

Rock Dove, *Columba livia* ____ ____ ____ ____

White-crowned Pigeon, *Columba leucocephala* ____ ____ ____ ____

Mourning Dove, *Zenaida macroura* ____ ____ ____ ____

Common Ground-Dove, *Columbina passerina* ____ ____ ____ ____

CUCKOOS AND ROADRUNNERS

Black-billed Cuckoo, *Coccyzus erythropthalmus* ____ ____ ____ ____

Yellow-billed Cuckoo, *Coccyzus americanus* ____ ____ ____ ____

Mangrove Cuckoo, *Coccyzus minor* ____ ____ ____ ____

Greater Roadrunner, *Geococcyx californianus* ____ ____ ____ ____

OWLS

Common Barn-Owl, *Tyto alba* ____ ____ ____ ____

Eastern Screech-Owl, *Otus asio* ____ ____ ____ ____

Great Horned Owl, *Bubo virginianus* ____ ____ ____ ____

Snowy Owl, *Nyctea scandiaca* ____ ____ ____ ____

Northern Hawk-Owl, *Surnia ulula* ____ ____ ____ ____

Burrowing Owl, *Athene cunicularia* ____ ____ ____ ____

Barred Owl, *Strix varia* ____ ____ ____ ____

Great Gray Owl, *Strix nebulosa* ____ ____ ____ ____

Long-eared Owl, *Asio otus* ____ ____ ____ ____

Short-eared Owl, *Asio flammeus* ____ ____ ____ ____

Boreal Owl, *Aegolius funereus* ____ ____ ____ ____

Northern Saw-whet Owl, *Aegolius acadicus* ____ ____ ____ ____

GOATSUCKERS AND ALLIES

Common Nighthawk, *Chordeiles minor* ____ ____ ____ ____

♂	♀	Juv.	Imm.	
—	—	—	—	Common Poorwill, *Phalaenoptilus nuttallii*
—	—	—	—	Chuck-will's-widow, *Caprimulgus carolinensis*
—	—	—	—	Whip-poor-will, *Caprimulgus vociferus*

SWIFTS AND HUMMINGBIRDS

♂	♀	Juv.	Imm.	
—	—	—	—	Chimney Swift, *Chaetura pelagica*
—	—	—	—	White-throated Swift, *Aeronautes saxatalis*
—	—	—	—	Ruby-throated Hummingbird, *Archilochus colubris*
—	—	—	—	Broad-tailed Hummingbird, *Selasphorus platycercus*

KINGFISHERS, WOODPECKERS, AND ALLIES

♂	♀	Juv.	Imm.	
—	—	—	—	Belted Kingfisher, *Ceryle alcyon*
—	—	—	—	Lewis' Woodpecker, *Melanerpes lewis*
—	—	—	—	Red-headed Woodpecker, *Melanerpes erythrocephalus*
♂	♀	Juv.	Imm.	Red-bellied Woodpecker, *Melanerpes carolinus*

♂	♀	Juv.	Imm.	
—	—	—	—	Yellow-bellied Sapsucker, *Sphyrapicus varius*
—	—	—	—	Downy Woodpecker, *Picoides pubescens*
—	—	—	—	Hairy Woodpecker, *Picoides villosus*
—	—	—	—	Red-cockaded Woodpecker, *Picoides borealis*
—	—	—	—	Three-toed Woodpecker, *Picoides tridactylus*
—	—	—	—	Black-backed Woodpecker, *Picoides arcticus*
—	—	—	—	Northern Flicker, *Colaptes auratus*
—	—	—	—	Pileated Woodpecker, *Dryocopus pileatus*

FLYCATCHERS

♂	♀	Juv.	Imm.	
—	—	—	—	Olive-sided Flycatcher, *Mionectes olivaceus*
—	—	—	—	Western Wood-Pewee, *Contopus sordidulus*
—	—	—	—	Eastern Wood-Pewee, *Contopus virens*
—	—	—	—	Yellow-bellied Flycatcher, *Empidonax flaviventris*
—	—	—	—	Acadian Flycatcher, *Empidonax virescens*

	♂ ♀ Juv. Imm.
Alder Flycatcher, *Empidonax alnorum*	— — — —
Willow Flycatcher, *Empidonax traillii*	— — — —
Least Flycatcher, *Empidonax minimus*	— — — —
Dusky Flycatcher, *Empidonax oberholseri*	— — — —
Western Flycatcher, *Empidonax difficilis*	— — — —
Eastern Phoebe, *Sayornis phoebe*	— — — —
Say's Phoebe, *Sayornis saya*	— — — —
Dusky-capped Flycatcher, *Myiarchus tuberculifer*	— — — —
Great Crested Flycatcher, *Myiarchus crinitus*	— — — —
Cassin's Kingbird, *Tyrannus vociferans*	— — — —
Western Kingbird, *Tyrannus verticalis*	— — — —
Eastern Kingbird, *Tyrannus tyrannus*	— — — —
Gray Kingbird, *Tyrannus dominicensis*	— — — —
Scissor-tailed Flycatcher, *Tyrannus forficatus*	— — — —

LARKS AND SWALLOWS

	♂ ♀ Juv. Imm.
Horned Lark, *Eremophila alpestris*	— — — —
Purple Martin, *Progne subis*	— — — —
Tree Swallow, *Tachycineta bicolor*	— — — —
Northern Rough-winged Swallow, *Stelgidopteryx ruficollis*	— — — —
Bank Swallow, *Riparia riparia*	— — — —
Cliff Swallow, *Hirundo pyrrhonota*	— — — —
Barn Swallow, *Hirundo rustica*	— — — —

JAYS, MAGPIES, AND CROWS

Gray Jay, *Perisoreus canadensis*	— — — —
Steller's Jay, *Cyanocitta stelleri*	— — — —
Blue Jay, *Cyanocitta cristata*	— — — —
Scrub Jay, *Aphelocoma coerulescens*	— — — —
Pinyon Jay, *Gymnorhinus cyanocephalus*	— — — —
Clark's Nutcracker, *Nucifraga columbiana*	— — — —

Black-billed Magpie, *Pica pica*

_ _ _ _ American Crow, *Corvus brachyrhynchos*

_ _ _ _ Fish Crow, *Corvus ossifragus*

Common Raven, *Corvus corax*

CHICKADEES AND TITMICE

_ _ _ _ Black-capped Chickadee, *Parus atricapillus*

_ _ _ _ Carolina Chickadee, *Parus carolinensis*

_ _ _ _ Boreal Chickadee, *Parus hudsonicus*

_ _ _ _ Tufted Titmouse, *Parus bicolor*

NUTHATCHES, CREEPERS, WRENS, AND DIPPERS

_ _ _ _ Red-breasted Nuthatch, *Sitta canadensis*

_ _ _ _ White-breasted Nuthatch, *Sitta carolinensis*

_ _ _ _ Brown-headed Nuthatch, *Sitta pusilla*

_ _ _ _ Brown Creeper, *Certhia americana*

_ _ _ _ Rock Wren, *Salpinctes obsoletus*

_ _ _ _ Canyon Wren, *Catherpes mexicanus*

_ _ _ _ Carolina Wren, *Thryothorus ludovicianus*

_ _ _ _ Bewick's Wren, *Thryomanes bewickii*

_ _ _ _ House Wren, *Troglodytes aedon*

_ _ _ _ Winter Wren, *Troglodytes troglodytes*

_ _ _ _ Sedge Wren, *Cistothorus platensis*

_ _ _ _ Marsh Wren, *Cistothorus palustris*

_ _ _ _ American Dipper, *Cinclus mexicanus*

KINGLETS, GNATCATCHERS, THRUSHES, AND ALLIES

_ _ _ _ Golden-crowned Kinglet, *Regulus satrapa*

_ _ _ _ Ruby-crowned Kinglet, *Regulus calendula*

_ _ _ _ Blue-gray Gnatcatcher, *Polioptila caerulea*

_ _ _ _ Northern Wheatear, *Oenanthe oenanthe*

_ _ _ _ Eastern Bluebird, *Sialia sialis*

	♂	♀	Juv.	Imm.
Mountain Bluebird, *Sialia currucoides*	—	—	—	—
Townsend's Solitaire, *Myadestes townsendi*	—	—	—	—
Veery, *Catharus fuscescens*	—	—	—	—
Gray-cheeked Thrush, *Catharus minimus*	—	—	—	—
Swainson's Thrush, *Catharus ustulatus*	—	—	—	—
Hermit Thrush, *Catharus guttatus*	—	—	—	—
Wood Thrush, *Hylocichla mustelina*	—	—	—	—
American Robin, *Turdus migratorius*	—	—	—	—

MOCKINGBIRDS, THRASHERS, AND PIPITS

	♂	♀	Juv.	Imm.
Gray Catbird, *Dumetella carolinensis*	—	—	—	—
Northern Mockingbird, *Mimus polyglottos*	—	—	—	—
Brown Thrasher, *Toxostoma rufum*	—	—	—	—
Water Pipit, *Anthus spinoletta*	—	—	—	—

WAXWINGS, SHRIKES, STARLINGS, AND VIREOS

	♂	♀	Juv.	Imm.
Bohemian Waxwing, *Bombycilla garrulus*	—	—	—	—
Cedar Waxwing, *Bombycilla cedrorum*	—	—	—	—
Northern Shrike, *Lanius excubitor*	—	—	—	—
Loggerhead Shrike, *Lanius ludovicianus*	—	—	—	—
European Starling, *Sturnus vulgaris*	—	—	—	—
White-eyed Vireo, *Vireo griseus*	—	—	—	—
Bell's Vireo, *Vireo bellii*	—	—	—	—
Solitary Vireo, *Vireo solitarius*	—	—	—	—
Yellow-throated Vireo, *Vireo flavifrons*	—	—	—	—
Warbling Vireo, *Vireo gilvus*	—	—	—	—
Philadelphia Vireo, *Vireo philadelphicus*	—	—	—	—
Red-eyed Vireo, *Vireo olivaceus*	—	—	—	—

WARBLERS

	♂	♀	Juv.	Imm.
Bachman's Warbler, *Vermivora bachmanii*	—	—	—	—
Blue-winged Warbler, *Vermivora pinus*	—	—	—	—

___ ___ ___ ___ Golden-winged
Warbler, *Vermivora
chrysoptera*

___ ___ ___ ___ Tennessee Warbler,
*Vermivora
peregrina*

___ ___ ___ ___ Orange-crowned
Warbler, *Vermivora
celata*

___ ___ ___ ___ Nashville Warbler,
*Vermivora
ruficapilla*

___ ___ ___ ___ Northern Parula,
Parula americana

___ ___ ___ ___ Yellow Warbler,
Dendroica petechia

___ ___ ___ ___ Chestnut-sided
Warbler, *Dendroica
pensylvanica*

___ ___ ___ ___ Magnolia Warbler,
*Dendroica
magnolia*

___ ___ ___ ___ Cape May Warbler,
Dendroica tigrina

___ ___ ___ ___ Black-throated Blue
Warbler, *Dendroica
caerulescens*

___ ___ ___ ___ Yellow-rumped
Warbler, *Dendroica
coronata*

___ ___ ___ ___ Black-throated
Green Warbler,
Dendroica virens

___ ___ ___ ___ Blackburnian
Warbler, *Dendroica
fusca*

___ ___ ___ ___ Yellow-throated
Warbler, *Dendroica
dominica*

___ ___ ___ ___ Pine Warbler,
Dendroica pinus

___ ___ ___ ___ Kirtland's Warbler,
*Dendroica
kirtlandii*

___ ___ ___ ___ Prairie Warbler,
Dendroica discolor

___ ___ ___ ___ Palm Warbler,
*Dendroica
palmarum*

___ ___ ___ ___ Bay-breasted
Warbler, *Dendroica
castanea*

___ ___ ___ ___ Blackpoll Warbler,
Dendroica striata

___ ___ ___ ___ Cerulean Warbler,
Dendroica cerulea

___ ___ ___ ___ Black-and-white
Warbler, *Mniotilta
varia*

___ ___ ___ ___ American Redstart,
Setophaga ruticilla

___ ___ ___ ___ Prothonotary
Warbler,
Protonotaria citrea

___ ___ ___ ___ Worm-eating
Warbler,
*Helmitheros
vermivorus*

___ ___ ___ ___ Swainson's Warbler,
*Limnothlypis
swainsonii*

___ ___ ___ ___ Ovenbird, *Seiurus
aurocapillus*

___ ___ ___ ___ Northern
Waterthrush,
*Seiurus
noveboracensis*

___ ___ ___ ___ Louisiana
Waterthrush,
Seiurus motacilla

___ ___ ___ ___ Kentucky Warbler,
*Oporornis
formosus*

	♂	♀	Juv.	Imm.

Connecticut Warbler, *Oporornis agilis* ___ ___ ___ ___

Mourning Warbler, *Oporornis philadelphia* ___ ___ ___ ___

Common Yellowthroat, *Geothlypis trichas* ___ ___ ___ ___

Hooded Warbler, *Wilsonia citrina* ___ ___ ___ ___

Wilson's Warbler, *Wilsonia pusilla* ___ ___ ___ ___

Canada Warbler, *Wilsonia canadensis* ___ ___ ___ ___

Yellow-breasted Chat, *Icteria virens* ___ ___ ___ ___

TANAGERS

Summer Tanager, *Piranga rubra* ___ ___ ___ ___

Scarlet Tanager, *Piranga olivacea* ___ ___ ___ ___

Western Tanager, *Piranga ludoviciana* ___ ___ ___ ___

CARDINALS AND GROSBEAKS

Northern Cardinal, *Cardinalis cardinalis* ___ ___ ___ ___

Rose-breasted Grosbeak, *Pheucticus ludovicianus* ___ ___ ___ ___

Black-headed Grosbeak, *Pheucticus melanocephalus* ___ ___ ___ ___

	♂	♀	Juv.	Imm.

Blue Grosbeak, *Guiraca caerulea* ___ ___ ___ ___

Lazuli Bunting, *Passerina amoena* ___ ___ ___ ___

Indigo Bunting, *Passerina cyanea* ___ ___ ___ ___

Painted Bunting, *Passerina ciris* ___ ___ ___ ___

Dickcissel, *Spiza americana* ___ ___ ___ ___

TOWHEES, SPARROWS, AND ALLIES

Green-tailed Towhee, *Pipilo chlorurus* ___ ___ ___ ___

Rufous-sided Towhee, *Pipilo erythrophthalmus* ___ ___ ___ ___

Bachman's Sparrow, *Aimophila aestivalis* ___ ___ ___ ___

Cassin's Sparrow, *Aimophila cassinii* ___ ___ ___ ___

Rufous-crowned Sparrow, *Aimophila ruficeps* ___ ___ ___ ___

American Tree Sparrow, *Spizella arborea* ___ ___ ___ ___

Chipping Sparrow, *Spizella passerina* ___ ___ ___ ___

Clay-colored Sparrow, *Spizella pallida* ___ ___ ___ ___

Field Sparrow, *Spizella pusilla* ___ ___ ___ ___

Vesper Sparrow, *Pooecetes gramineus* ___ ___ ___ ___

♂ ♀ Juv. Imm.

__ __ __ __ Lark Sparrow,
*Chondestes
grammacus*

__ __ __ __ Black-throated
Sparrow,
*Amphispiza
bilineata*

__ __ __ __ Lark Bunting,
*Calamospiza
melanocorys*

__ __ __ __ Savannah Sparrow,
*Passerculus
sandwichensis*

__ __ __ __ Baird's Sparrow,
*Ammodramus
bairdii*

__ __ __ __ Grasshopper
Sparrow,
*Ammodramus
savannarum*

__ __ __ __ Henslow's Sparrow,
*Ammodramus
henslowii*

__ __ __ __ LeConte's Sparrow,
*Ammodramus
leconteii*

__ __ __ __ Sharp-tailed
Sparrow,
*Ammodramus
caudacutus*

__ __ __ __ Seaside Sparrow,
*Ammodramus
maritimus*

__ __ __ __ Fox Sparrow,
Passerella iliaca

__ __ __ __ Song Sparrow,
Melospiza melodia

__ __ __ __ Lincoln's Sparrow,
Melospiza lincolnii

__ __ __ __ Swamp Sparrow,
*Melospiza
georgiana*

♂ ♀ Juv. Imm.

__ __ __ __ White-throated
Sparrow,
*Zonotrichia
albicollis*

__ __ __ __ White-crowned
Sparrow,
*Zonotrichia
leucophrys*

__ __ __ __ Harris' Sparrow,
*Zonotrichia
querula*

__ __ __ __ Dark-eyed Junco,
Junco hyemalis

__ __ __ __ McCown's
Longspur,
*Calcarius
mccownii*

__ __ __ __ Lapland Longspur,
*Calcarius
lapponicus*

__ __ __ __ Smith's Longspur,
Calcarius pictus

__ __ __ __ Chestnut-collared
Longspur,
Calcarius ornatus

__ __ __ __ Snow Bunting,
*Plectrophenax
nivalis*

MEADOWLARKS, BLACKBIRDS, AND ORIOLES

__ __ __ __ Bobolink,
*Dolichonyx
oryzivorus*

__ __ __ __ Red-winged
Blackbird, *Agelaius
phoeniceus*

__ __ __ __ Eastern
Meadowlark,
Sturnella magna

	♂	♀	Juv.	Imm.
Western Meadowlark, *Sturnella neglecta*	—	—	—	—
Yellow-headed Blackbird, *Xanthocephalus xanthocephalus*	—	—	—	—
Rusty Blackbird, *Euphagus carolinus*	—	—	—	—
Brewer's Blackbird, *Euphagus cyanocephalus*	—	—	—	—
Great-tailed Grackle, *Quiscalus mexicanus*	—	—	—	—
Boat-tailed Grackle, *Quiscalus major*	—	—	—	—
Common Grackle, *Quiscalus quiscula*	—	—	—	—
Brown-headed Cowbird, *Molothrus ater*	—	—	—	—
Orchard Oriole, *Icterus spurius*	—	—	—	—
Northern Oriole, *Icterus galbula*	—	—	—	—

FINCHES AND ALLIES

	♂	♀	Juv.	Imm.
Rosy Finch, *Leucosticte arctoa*	—	—	—	—
Pine Grosbeak, *Pinicola enucleator*	—	—	—	—
Purple Finch, *Carpodacus purpureus*	—	—	—	—
House Finch, *Carpodacus mexicanus*	—	—	—	—

	♂	♀	Juv.	Imm.
Red Crossbill, *Loxia curvirostra*	—	—	—	—
White-winged Crossbill, *Loxia leucoptera*	—	—	—	—
Common Redpoll, *Carduelis flammea*	—	—	—	—
Hoary Redpoll, *Carduelis hornemanni*	—	—	—	—
Pine Siskin, *Carduelis pinus*	—	—	—	—
Lesser Goldfinch, *Carduelis psaltria*	—	—	—	—
American Goldfinch, *Carduelis tristis*	—	—	—	—
Evening Grosbeak, *Coccothraustes verpertinus*	—	—	—	—
House Sparrow, *Passer domesticus*	—	—	—	—

The
Maps

Following are selected geographic range maps for some of the more commonly seen species of the region as well as more uncommon species, to show divergent patterns. Included here are maps showing distribution for breeding, wintering, and resident ranges. It should be noted that no range map can be entirely definitive, and those included here provide general parameters of geographic ranges for selected species.

Resident species are defined as those that are nonmigratory. These are birds that regularly reside in a given area. The distribution of the migratory species is described as either "breeding" or "wintering," in that the bird is usually in one or the other locale during the year. In some cases, the species may be in the same locale both when it is breeding and wintering, or the ranges may overlap. The maps that follow indicate the activities of various species only within our range, that is, east of the 100th meridian in North America.

Additionally, it is important to remember that a species will be found only in appropriate habitats within its range. It should be noted that our winter is actually summer for visiting seabirds that winter south of the equator.

Colors and patterns are used on these maps to distinguish species and behavior. For the most part, two species are shown on a single map, each species indicated by the use of an individual color. The varying patterns on the maps indicate the different ranges of particular activities, such as breeding, wintering, or resident status, of a bird. A wintering range is shown by the use of a lined pattern, whereas a dot pattern indicates the breeding locale of the species. A tone of the species' color shows resident ranges. Sometimes a third color (purple or orange) may be created. Rather than indicate a third bird's activity, it is indicative of overlapping ranges of activity of two birds. In addition, the order of the maps that follow corresponds to the taxonomic order of bird species.

Range and distribution information is often very useful in making a definitive identification, and should be used in conjunction with other identifying techniques whenever possible. Very often a bird can be eliminated as the one having been assumed to have been sighted because it does not conform to the known range or behaviors of the presumed sighted species.

. . . .

Maps read
left to right;
labels read
top to bottom

Breeding

Wintering

Resident

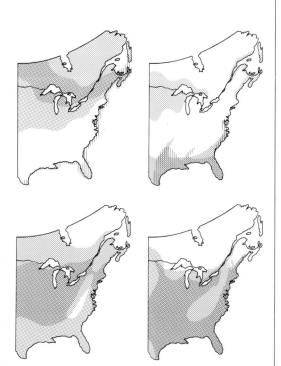

Common
Loon

Pied-billed
Grebe

Double-crested
Cormorant

Anhinga

American
Bittern

Least
Bittern

Green-backed
Heron

Black-crowned
Night-Heron

Glossy Ibis

Snow Goose ●

Green-winged Teal ●

Blue-winged Teal ●

American Black Duck ●

Gadwall ●

Mallard ●

Northern Harrier ●

Sharp-shinned Hawk ●

Cooper's Hawk ●

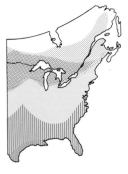

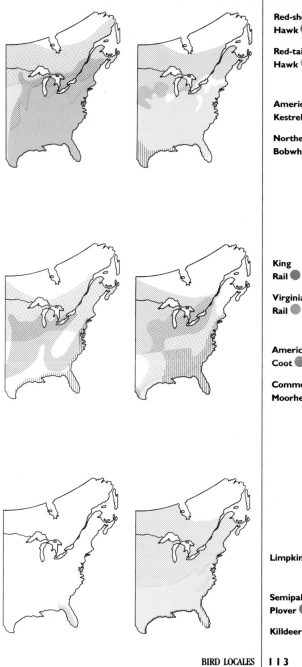

Red-shouldered Hawk

Red-tailed Hawk

American Kestrel

Northern Bobwhite

King Rail

Virginia Rail

American Coot

Common Moorhen

Limpkin

Semipalmated Plover

Killdeer

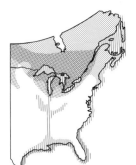 

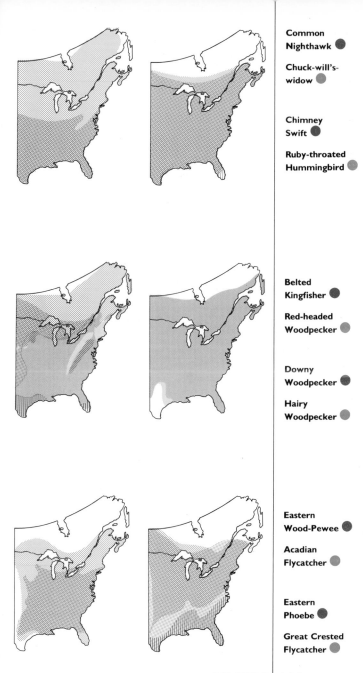

Common Nighthawk

Chuck-will's-widow

Chimney Swift

Ruby-throated Hummingbird

Belted Kingfisher

Red-headed Woodpecker

Downy Woodpecker

Hairy Woodpecker

Eastern Wood-Pewee

Acadian Flycatcher

Eastern Phoebe

Great Crested Flycatcher

Eastern Kingbird ●

Gray Kingbird ●

Purple Martin ●

Tree Swallow ●

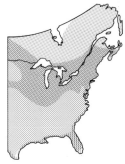

Northern Rough-winged Swallow ●

Bank Swallow ●

Barn Swallow ○

Blue Jay ●

Scrub Jay ●

American Crow ●

Common Raven ●

Black-capped Chickadee ●

Carolina Chickadee ●

Tufted
Titmouse

White-breasted
Nuthatch

Red-breasted
Nuthatch

Brown Creeper

Carolina
Wren

House
Wren

Golden-crowned
Kinglet

Blue-gray
Gnatcatcher

Eastern
Bluebird

Gray-cheeked
Thrush

Wood
Thrush

American
Robin

Gray Catbird ●

Northern Mockingbird ●

Brown Thrasher ●

Cedar Waxwing ●

Loggerhead Shrike ●

European Starling ●

White-eyed Vireo ●

Solitary Vireo ●

Yellow-throated Vireo ●

Warbling Vireo ●

Red-eyed Vireo ●

Northern Parula ●

Yellow Warbler ●

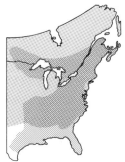

THE MAPS

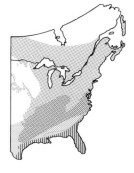

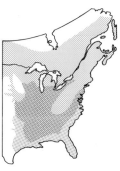
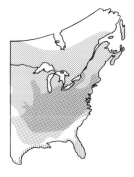

Scarlet Tanager

Rose-breasted Grosbeak

Blue Grosbeak

 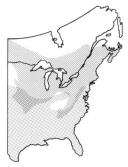

Indigo Bunting

Dickcissel

Rufous-sided Towhee

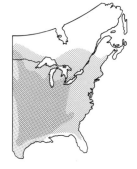 

American Tree Sparrow

Chipping Sparrow

Field Sparrow

Vesper Sparrow

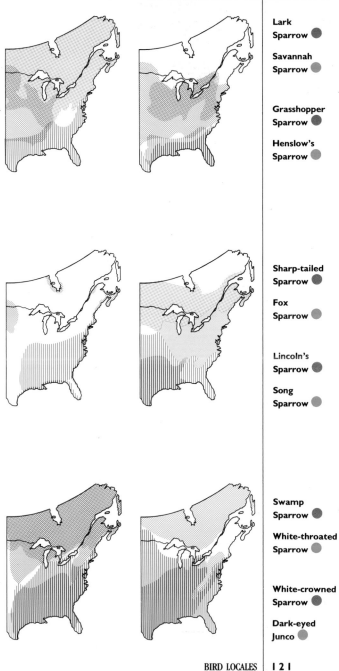

Lark
Sparrow ●

Savannah
Sparrow ●

Grasshopper
Sparrow ●

Henslow's
Sparrow ●

Sharp-tailed
Sparrow ●

Fox
Sparrow ●

Lincoln's
Sparrow ●

Song
Sparrow ●

Swamp
Sparrow ●

White-throated
Sparrow ●

White-crowned
Sparrow ●

Dark-eyed
Junco ●

Red-winged Blackbird ●

Rusty Blackbird ●

Brown-headed Cowbird ●

Orchard Oriole ●

Northern (Baltimore) Oriole ●

Purple Finch ●

House Finch ●

Pine Siskin ●

American Goldfinch ●

Eastern Meadowlark ●

Competitions

Contact the following organizations for information:

Big Day
American Birding Association
618 Lavaca
Austin, TX 78701
(512) 474–4804

Christmas Bird Count
% C.B.C. Editor
American Birds
National Audubon Society
950 Third Avenue
New York, NY 10022
(212) 832–3200

The World Series of Birding
% Mr. Peter Dunne
Scherman/Hawkman
  Sanctuary
New Jersey Audubon Society
P.O. Box 693
Bernardsville, NJ 07924
(201) 766–5787

Audubon, Ornithological, and Naturalist Societies

UNITED STATES

. . . .

N A T I O N A L

American Birding Association
618 Lavaca
Austin, TX 78701
(512) 474–4804

American Ornithologists Union
% National Museum of
  Natural History
Smithsonian Institution
10th and Constitution Avenue
  Northwest
Washington, D.C. 20560
(202) 357–2051

International Council for Bird Preservation
645 Pennsylvania Avenue
  Southeast
Washington, D.C. 20003
(202) 547–9009

National Audubon Society
950 Third Avenue
New York, NY 10022
(212) 832–3200

National Audubon Society Rare Bird Alert
950 Third Avenue
New York, NY 10022
(212) 832–3200

. . . .

S T A T E

Contact these societies for local chapters:

Connecticut Audubon Society
2325 Burr Street
Fairfield, CT 06430
(203) 259–6305

Florida Audubon Society
1101 Audubon Way
Maitland, FL 32651
(305) 647–2615

Hawaii Audubon Society
P.O. Box 22832
Honolulu, HI 96822

Illinois Audubon Society
P.O. Box 608
Wayne, IL 60184
(312) 584–6290

Indiana Audubon Society
Mary Gray Bird Sanctuary
RR6
Connersville, IN 47331
(317) 825–9788

Maine Audubon Society
Gilsland Farm
118 Route 1
Falmouth, ME 04105
(207) 781–2330

**Massachusetts Audubon
Society, Inc.**
South Great Road
Lincoln, MA 01773
(617) 259–9500

Michigan Audubon Society
409 West E. Avenue
Kalamazoo, MI 49007
(616) 344–8648

**Audubon Society of New
Hampshire**
3 Silk Farm Road
P.O. Box 528B
Concord, NH 03301
(603) 244–9909

**New Jersey Audubon
Society**
790 Ewing Avenue
P.O. Box 125
Franklin Lake, NJ 07417
(201) 891–1211

**Audubon Society of Rhode
Island**
40 Bowen Street
Providence, RI 02903
(401) 521–1670

C A N A D A

. . . .

N A T I O N A L

**Canadian Nature
Federation**
75 Albert Street, Suite 203
Ottawa, ON K1P 6G1
(613) 238–6154

Canadian Wildlife Service
Environment Canada
Ottawa, ON K1A OE7
(819) 997–1301
(819) 997–1686
  (publications)

. . . .

R E G I O N A L

**Federation of Ontario
Naturalists**
355 Lesmill Road
Don Mills, ON M3B 2W8
(416) 444–2553

**Manitoba Naturalists
Society**
128 James Avenue,
  Room 302
Winnipeg, MN R3B ON8
(204) 943–9029

**Ottawa Field
Naturalists Club**
Box 3264
Postal Station C
Ottawa, ON K1Y 4J5
(613) 722–3050

Periodicals

UNITED STATES

Audubon
National Audubon Society
950 Third Avenue
New York, NY 10022
(212) 832-3200
*bimonthly publication free
    with membership*

The Auk
American Ornithologists
    Union
c/o National Museum of
    Natural History
Smithsonian Institution
10th and Constitution Avenue
    Northwest
Washington, D.C. 20560
(202) 357-2051

Birding
American Birding Association
P.O. Box 4335
Austin, TX 78765
(512) 474-4804
bimonthly

The Living Bird Quarterly
Laboratory of Ornithology at
    Cornell University
159 Sapsucker Woods Road
Ithaca, NY 14850
(607) 255-7317
free with membership

. . . .

CANADA

*These publications cover all
aspects of wildlife
preservation*

The Canadian Field Naturalist
Ottawa Field Naturalists Club
Box 3264
Postal Station C
Ottawa, ON KIY 4J5
(613) 722-3050

Nature Canada
Canada Nature Federation
75 Albert Street
Ottawa, ON K1P 6G1
(613) 238-6154

Seasons
Federation of Ontario
Naturalists
355 Lesmill Road
Don Mills, ON M3B 2W8
(416) 444-8419

Books

*The A.O.U. Check-list of
North American Birds,* 6th
ed. Lawrence, Kans.: Allen
Press Inc., 1983.

Farrand, John, ed. *The
Audubon Society Master
Guide to Birding.* 3 vols.
New York: Knopf, 1984.

*National Geographic
Society's Field Guide to the
Birds of North America.*
Washington, D.C.: National
Geographic Society, 1983.

Peterson, Roger Tory. *A Field
Guide to the Birds East of
the Rockies,* 4th ed. Boston:
Houghton Mifflin Co., 1980.

_____ . *A Field Guide to
Western Birds,* 2d ed.
Boston: Houghton Mifflin Co.,
1961.

Robbins, Chandler S., et al.
Birds of North America, rev.
ed. Racine, Wis.: Western
Publishers, 1983.